Congress Oversees the Bureaucracy

MORRIS S. OGUL

CONGRESS
Oversees the Bureaucracy
Studies in Legislative Supervision

University of Pittsburgh Press

Library of Congress Cataloging in Publication Data

Ogul, Morris S   birth date
Congress oversees the bureaucracy.

Bibliography: p. 219
Includes index.
1. United States. Congress. 2. United States
—Executive departments. I. Title.
JK585.048   328.73'07'456   75-33546
ISBN 0-8229-3313-6   ISBN 0-8229-5288-2 pbk.

Material from *On Capitol Hill* by John Bibby and Roger Davidson (Dryden Press, 1967) is reprinted by permission of Holt, Rinehart and Winston, Inc. Excerpts from Gerald Cullinan, *The United States Postal Service*, © 1973 by Praeger Publishers, Inc., New York, excerpted and reprinted by permission. Material from *Congress in Crisis: Politics and Congressional Reform* by Roger H. Davidson, David M. Kovenock, and Michael K. O'Leary, © 1966 by Wadsworth Publishing Company, Inc., Belmont, California 94002, reprinted by permission of the publisher, Duxbury Press. Excerpts from *The Legislative Process in the United States* by Malcolm E. Jewell and Samuel C. Patterson, © copyright, 1966, by Random House, Inc., and *The Political Process* by J. Leiper Freeman, rev. ed., © copyright, 1955, 1965, by Random House, Inc., are reprinted by permission of the publisher. Material from *History of the House of Representatives*, copyright © 1961 by George B. Galloway, is reprinted by permission of the publisher, Thomas Y. Crowell Company, Inc. Material from Kenneth E. Gray, "Congressional Interference in Administration," Elazar et al. (Eds.), *Cooperation and Conflict: Readings in American Federalism*, 1969, p. 525, reproduced by permission of the publisher, F. E. Peacock Publishers, Inc., Itasca, Illinois. Excerpts from Carl Kaysen, "Data Banks and Dossiers," *The Public Interest*, Number 7 (Spring 1967), 3, copyright © 1967 by National Affairs, Inc., reprinted by permission.
     Material from the *New York Times* © 1969/68/67 by the New York Times Company. Reprinted by permission. Material from the *Washington Post* © 1969 by the *Washington Post*. Reprinted by permission.

To the memory of Jack and Sarah Ogul

Contents

List of Tables   ix

Preface   xi

1. Legislative Oversight: Theory and Practice   3

2. The House Post Office and Civil Service
   Committee   27

3. The Post Office and Civil Service Committee:
   Member Priorities and Oversight   56

4. The Special Subcommittee on the Invasion of
   Privacy   92

5. The House Judiciary Committee: Subcommittee
   Five   129

6. Oversight as a Latent and a Manifest Function   153

7. Legislative Oversight in the Present and in the
   Future   181

Notes   205

Bibliography   219

Index   233

Tables

1. House Members with Single Committee Assignments   59
2. Postal Employee Organizations' Periodicals   67
3. Expenditures Reported by Post Office Lobbyists   75
4. Expenditures of the SSIP   94
5. Committee Assignments for Members of Judiciary Subcommittee Five   139
6. Reports to Be Made by the Executive Departments to the Congress   177
7. Expenditures by Select, Special, and Standing Congressional Committees for Investigations   194

Preface

My desire to do research on congressional oversight of the federal bureaucracy sprang in 1964 from a rather orthodox scholarly motivation: a belief that the importance of the subject far exceeded the attention given to it. Evidence from the decade since has accentuated the significance of the subject matter; scholars, in the main, have continued to practice benign neglect.

The active phase of this research began in the summers of 1965 and 1966 with interviews in Washington, D.C. The data and analysis in this study are based on a combination of these interviews (some eighty-nine in total) with the written materials that relate to them. Following what has come to be a canon of congressional interviewing, interviewees, when quoted directly, are seldom cited by name. All unattributed quotations are from these interviews with congressmen, congressional staff members, interest-group representatives, and high-level bureaucrats.

In research of this scope, one develops more debts than can be acknowledged. Financial support for the interviewing process came from the Carnegie Corporation through the Study of Congress sponsored by the American Political Science Association. Many congressmen, the staff persons in their offices, and those working for congressional committees gave generously of their time. They pointed the way to valuable sources, both written and human. Not all of the interviewees will agree with my interpretations. They can be assured that their views were always carefully considered.

Several persons in Washington deserve special mention. Congressman William S. Moorhead and his able staff provided more help than assisting a constituent demanded. The efficiency and good cheer of his administrative assistant, Mollie D. Cohen, merits greater recognition than mention in a preface. Richard Barton, professional staff member of the House Post Office and Civil Service Committee, suggested an unusual number of fruitful leads.

Many dedicated and energetic graduate assistants helped move the research forward. The major contributors were Louise Royster Brown, Barbara Laughlin Mann, James Olp, Lynette Perkins, and Mary Ann Vitaro. The final typing was done by Linda Perkins and Kendall Stanley.

Holbert N. Carroll and William J. Keefe each read parts of the manuscript. I am sure that the wisdom they gave exceeded the advice taken. I thank them for what they did. Unfortunately, I cannot blame any shortcomings of the study on them. My wife, Eleanor, suffered the pains reserved for wives of writing husbands. In addition, she assisted with transcribing the tapes of interview notes and with typing the preliminary drafts.

The staff of the University of Pittsburgh Press provided a hospitable environment for publication. I wish to thank Frederick A. Hetzel, Director, and Louise Craft, Editor, for this. My special appreciation goes to Beth E. Luey, whose keen eye detected an embarrassing number of superfluous words and awkward phrases. This book is a better one because of her efforts.

Congress Oversees the Bureaucracy

Chapter 1 Legislative Oversight: Theory and Practice

The question of who rules the rulers is as old as political philosophy and as new as tomorrow's newspaper headlines. The classic answer in the United States—the people rule—seems so out of accord with the realities of the twentieth century that alternative answers need to be sought. If the people do not rule directly, then perhaps the rulers restrain one another. This more realistic assessment, symbolized in American politics in such slogans as "the separation of powers" and "checks and balances," does not capture all of reality, but it does suggest topics especially worthy of attention. One of the most substantial of these is how the president and the bureaucracy relate to the Congress. For it is in these interactions that many see a primary defense against oligarchy or tyranny.

The simplest and least useful definition of executive-legislative relations holds that the Congress makes the laws and the president and his subordinates carry them out. A more complex and accurate view suggests that the administration proposes most important policies and the Congress reacts by accepting, amending, or rejecting them. The executive branch then implements them. Agenda-setting and policy initiative flow regularly from the executive. Those who assert the decline of the Congress as a viable political competitor cite this fact as evidence to support their position.

Many observers of the Congress discern legislative oversight of the bureaucracy as one means by which competitive leadership can remain a reality in American politics. Even those who question the ability of the Congress to legislate independently often believe that the Congress can perform the key function of overseeing the conduct of the national bureaucracy.

For many reasons, researchers have tended to slight this dimension of executive-legislative relations. Despite its perceived importance, oversight has remained a stepchild; a dearth of analysis is reality. As John Saloma put it, "Congressional participation in, and 'oversight' or review of, the administrative process in government is one of the least understood functions that Congress performs."[1] The significance of the topic provides ample justification for additional attention.

This book attempts to shed some light on congressional oversight of the national bureaucracy. This is its broad purpose. The particular questions to be explored are: Why is it that the Congress acts as it does in its efforts to oversee? And what does the Congress accomplish by its efforts? The oversight behavior of three committees and subcommittees of the House of Representatives in the period 1965–1966 will be probed intensively. These specific case studies will buttress the analysis about the vexing problems of oversight generally.

Does the Congress Do Enough?

The Congress oversees formally and informally in many ways on a daily basis. It does this selectively. The most visible and perhaps the most effective way is through the appropriations process; the most unnoticed occurs as it considers authorizations, performs casework, and goes about business not directly labeled as oversight.

What this activity accomplishes is not as clear. Opinions about the adequacy of congressional oversight vary. Some critics assert that oversight is minimal. For others, congressional oversight is seen as so pervasive as to cripple the effective functioning of departments and agencies. Whether behavior is adequate is a complex question, for what is adequate depends on what is expected.

The clearest single statement about the oversight that the law requires the Congress to perform comes from that often quoted and seldom heeded statement in the Legislative Reorganization Act of 1946 assigning each standing committee the responsibility to "exercise continuous watchfulness of the execution by the administrative agencies concerned of any laws, the subject matter of which is within the jurisdiction of such committee." There seems to be consensus in the Congress on the principle that extensive and systematic oversight *ought* to be conducted.

That expectation is simply not met. One reason lies in the nature of the expectation. The plain but seldom acknowledged fact is that this task, at least as defined above, is impossible to perform. No amount of congressional dedication and energy, no conceivable increase in the size of committee staffs, and no extraordinary boost in committee budgets will enable the Congress to carry out its oversight obligations in a comprehensive and systematic manner. The job is too large for any combination of members and staff to master completely. Congressmen who feel obligated to obey the letter of the law are doomed to feelings of inadequacy and frustration.

Assessment of whether oversight is sufficient is tied to preferences and choices in three areas: policy preferences on substantive policy issues; definitions of what oversight is; and preferred models of legislative behavior.

Substantive Policy Preferences

Policy preferences and attitudes toward oversight frequently relate in painfully obvious ways. For some, judgments about process are routinely a function of substantive policy preferences. These persons endorse whatever structure or procedure promotes their policy desires at the moment. If a policy position draws its support from the Congress, then extensive and systematic oversight is deemed crucial; if the executive branch most adequately articulates one's policy preferences, then congressmen are deemed badgering bunglers who impose barriers to rational decision-making.

In the controversy over United States involvement in Vietnam in the 1960s, for instance, some strong supporters of presidential prerogatives in foreign affairs turned into congressional partisans as they found their policy preferences reflected more in the behavior of key senators than in the presidency. Judgments about institutions and processes are frequently functions of substantive policy positions. As Seymour Scher put it, "For the committee member there was no abstract meaning in the term 'proper' when used to describe the relationship between the independent commission and the committee. Anything was proper that served to bring the agency . . . into accord with the member's view of how the agency should act."[2]

One close observer of the Congress reached a stronger conclusion: Members seldom even reflect on questions of process outside the context of particular policies and problems. "Our impression is that members have little time and few occasions to reflect on the process. Only when the process itself becomes a policy issue as it did in the post war debates culminating in the Monroney-LaFollette Act and the reorganization of Congress, do members have opportunity to give much thought to such questions."[3]

Definitions

Assessment of oversight is conditioned also by one's perception of what oversight is. If oversight is defined only in terms of formal powers, different conclusions emerge about its adequacy than if informal relationships are taken into account. Those who view oversight as simply an attempt to influence the implementation of legislation through post-statutory investigations will reach different conclusions than will those who are sensitive to oversight performed latently.

How oversight is defined affects what oversight one finds. Writers assess oversight differently at times because they are not talking about the same thing. These differences are also mirrored in vocabulary. Thus the words scrutiny, review, inspection, control, command, supervision, watchfulness, and influence each carry connotations about what is expected.

The Joint Committee on the Organization of Congress worried at some length about appropriate terminology to describe the oversight function. Part of this groping reflected competing conceptions of reality. Their choice of "review" to replace "oversight" clarified very little.

Models of Legislative Behavior

What we expect the Congress to do conditions how we assess congressional behavior. Students of legislative oversight build on implicit or explicit value models. The following statement from the *Record* of the Bar Association of the city of New York deftly illustrates this point: "Every effort should be made to insure that confirmation hearings are not made the occasion for bringing pressure to bear on an agency in a policy area."[4]

Or, contrast the arguments of Joseph Harris and Charles Hyneman. Harris argues that the task of the legislature is to set broad standards and to leave implementation within these broad confines to the administrators. "However, legislatures should not—and by their very nature cannot—undertake detailed supervision of administration or effectively substitute their judgments for those of executive officials in all matters."[5] Hyneman, on the other hand, asserts that if Congress is to perform its representative function adequately, it should set as many of the details of bureaucratic action as its desires and capacity permit:

While there is no way of finding a "right answer" to the question as to how much detail is desirable, it is possible to identify certain considerations which point to where a satisfactory answer will be found. . . .

First, and fundamental, is the rule that Congress should specify in the statute every guide, every condition, every statement of principle that it knows in advance it wants to have applied in the situations that are expected to arise. This rule derives from a concept of legislative supremacy. It is based on the conviction that Congress, being the nation's representative assembly, ought to have authority to provide in law for anything that it wants any part of the government to do, so long as it does not violate a prohibition of the constitution. . . . If Congress is to have the supreme authority to say what the government is to do, then it must be in a position to describe what it wants done in as much detail as it thinks necessary.[6]

Students of legislative oversight, like most people, are in part prisoners of the pictures in their heads. What we see is partly a function of what we would like to see. What this may mean in practice is shown in the following chart adapted from materials in *Congress in Crisis*.[7] Three widely held views of how the Congress should function are set forth in the left-hand column. The column on the right shows the view of oversight that flows from each expectation.

Theory of Congressional Functions	Consequences for Oversight
The president and congress are equals with coordinate powers (Literary Theory, pp. 17–25).	Congressional oversight of the executive should be facilitated through increased use of detailed committee review of legis-

	lation, appointments, and appropriations (p. 25).
The president initiates; congress reacts and ratifies (Executive Force Theory, pp. 25–31).	Congress should grant relatively broad mandates to executive agencies and should cease such harassing tactics as one-year authorizations or required committee clearances for certain executive actions (p. 31).
Executive force theory plus cohesive, responsible political parties (Party Government Theory, pp. 31–34).	Same as executive force theory (p. 33).

In sum, policy preferences, definitions, and models of behavior all shape assessments of the adequacy of the performance of the oversight function.

Research on Legislative Oversight

Anyone attempting to understand the conduct of legislative oversight of the bureaucracy finds relatively little help in the writing about it. Two reasons may be suggested. First, there has been relatively little research on the subject. Second, most of the material published has been concerned primarily with assessing the quality of oversight or in providing descriptions of formal procedures.

The pitfalls of these approaches are illustrated in the study entitled *Congressional Control of Administration*. In this work, politics is perceived as peripheral. At worst, politics is viewed as an aberration from sound principles of executive-legislative relations.[8] The intrusion of politics into oversight is acknowledged begrudgingly at best.

In recent years, the research of scholars such as John F. Bibby, J. Leiper Freeman, Seymour Scher, and Dale Vinyard has pointed in a different direction.[9] Politics has moved from aberration to essence. The implicit governing assumption in this research is that oversight is most meaningfully discussed as an integral part of the political process. This movement is from a primary concern with a priori principles to a concern with analyses designed to cope with the full complexities of legislative behavior. Put another way, normative judgment and simple description have given way as primary objectives to political analysis. The present research is in the mainstream of this newer trend which assumes that a study of the conditions accounting for oversight activity or inactivity is surely a useful and probably a necessary precondition to statements about the adequacy of oversight and especially, if one is dissatisfied, to proposals for what to do about what one finds.

A review of the analytically oriented studies reveals that oversight is neither comprehensive nor systematic. Oversight is performed intermittently. The Congress oversees essentially through its committees and subcommittees, only a few of which have been carefully studied. Moreover, oversight has been studied primarily as a manifest function—hence the conclusion that little is performed. Awareness of the performance of oversight as a latent function leads to a fuller understanding of the process. In addition to extending existing research, this study will probe into some problems in the translation of role expectations into role behavior. Finally, this study seeks to relate the growing body of studies on committees in the Congress to studies on legislative oversight.

If all oversight is conceived as an integral part of the legislative process, explained by variables relevant for other legislative behavior, then one should not treat it as an isolated phenomenon. For example, the analysis developed in this research, although organized differently, is compatible with that of Richard F. Fenno, Jr., in his trailblazing volume, *Congressmen in Committees.*[10] Fenno argues that committee behavior can be explained by attention to the goals of committee members and to the environmental constraints within which the committee functions.

A first step toward analysis is to provide an explicit statement of the subject matter. For purposes of this study, the following working definition will be used: *Legislative oversight is behavior by legislators and their staffs, individually or collectively, which results in an impact, intended or not, on bureaucratic behavior.* The focus is on what congressmen do and why. Hence conventional distinctions such as those between legislation and oversight, hearings and investigations are ignored in favor of an approach which seeks out oversight behavior wherever performed throughout the legislative process and searches for the conditions associated with its presence.

Opportunity Factors

Oversight is most likely if a series of conditioning factors is present. These are called opportunity factors because in their absence, one can predict that little oversight will occur.

Opportunity factors enhance or lessen the potential for oversight irrespective of any single, concrete situation. They establish a presumptive case for the possibility of substantial oversight. However, the presence of intervening variables will weaken attempts at establishing direct linkages between opportunity factors and behavior. Analysis of opportunity factors points to the conditions under which a high proclivity toward oversight will exist. These factors taken together provide an oversight-inducing syndrome. Opportunity factors tend to promote the potential for oversight or to limit the possibility of it. Seven such factors may be identified.

Legal Authority
Most obvious of the opportunity factors in the legal authority of the Congress and its committees. The lawmaking

authority of the Congress leads by implication into attempts to oversee the implementation of the law. The authority over government expenditures may stimulate efforts to see that the money appropriated is used as intended by the Congress. The legal division of labor among congressional committees promotes the attention of subunits of the Congress to subunits of the bureaucracy. The provision of the Legislative Reorganization Act of 1946 assigning each standing committee a responsibility to "exercise continuous watchfulness of the execution by the administrative agencies concerned of any laws, the subject matter of which is within the jurisdiction of such committee" provides an adequate legal base for almost any efforts at oversight.

Law legitimates substantial oversight activity by the Congress. But in a few situations, the absence of such authority can be a handicap to effective oversight.[11] In general, the legal power of legislatures to oversee is a relevant but rarely decisive factor in explaining behavior. Authority is normally larger than its exercise. What seems to matter more is the combination of a desire to oversee and resources to do so.

A Senate Committee staff member pointed out:

> *In some cases, committee staff members or congressmen themselves ask for material from the General Accounting Office that they had received at some previous time and had discarded. Now, because of new sets of circumstances and new interests on their part and because of new axes to grind, they ask for the material. They ask for it again, not because it suggested things to them originally, but rather because they* now *have a use for it.*

Legal capacity and a vague sense of obligation provide an inadequate explanation of oversight activities. Oversight flows more from concrete felt needs than from general obligations, legal or otherwise.

Evidence in support of these generalizations is found in the testimony of former Senator A. S. "Mike" Monroney concerning twenty years of experience with the legal obligation to oversee contained in the Legislative Reorganization Act of 1946: "But we find ourselves bogged down in an impossible situation where this regular committee oversight of the bureaus and departments under its jurisdiction is not carried out to any degree whatever."[12]

Staff Resources

A second opportunity factor is that of staff resources for congressional decision makers. Access to staff and the willingness to use it are often important preconditions to substantial oversight. Oversight without effective staff work is normally impossible. But the amount of oversight performed does not depend mainly on the size of the staff available. Adequate staff is a necessary precondition to oversight but is not a sufficient one.[13] Other factors such as member priorities seem more basic. As John F. Manley notes, "They [the staff] take more cues from the formal policy makers than they give."[14]

The comments of a highly regarded staff member of a Senate committee support a related point:

> Basically the staff responds to member requests and member pressures instead of generating masses of material that might be ignored. When I first came on the committee as a staff member, I prepared many studies. Other staff people did the same. Our general idea was to do exhaustive work to prepare background materials that the members could later use for investigations and other purposes. We would work for six months on a project, spend hours and hours on it, and then it would come before the committee to be considered for investigation. One committee member would say, "Oh, there is nothing here. Let's forget it." After many experiences of this sort, the staff adopted a more passive role. The staff essentially works on the proposition that it will respond to member pressures.

Professional staff members will usually mirror the policy and process orientations of the congressmen who hire them and direct their behavior. A chairman passive about oversight is unlikely to have professional staff members who give it top priority. The senior minority member on a committee may regard the oversight function as unimportant, or he may lessen his efforts in exchange for benefits derived from the majority. The minority staff members then tend to reflect his views. Other factors can outweigh partisan opposition.

Subject Matter

A third opportunity factor is the subject matter of a policy or program. The more technical and complex the subject matter is perceived to be, the less the likelihood of oversight. Only a few members of the Congress are experts in *any* area of bureaucratic operations. Those who are, master very few. Fulfilling the obligations of a congressman requires more time than a member has available. Ease of immersion into a subject will then be one factor governing his activity. What is particularly important is how complex the subject seems to the participants involved.

How a subject area is organized within the executive branch also shapes oversight. An activity centered in one agency or department may be much easier to follow than one spread over several departments and agencies. According to one staff member:

> *Beyond those factors related to the time and energy and inclinations of the congressional committees themselves, the dispersal of programs in the executive department raises problems of oversight. A committee which passes a bill concerned with a given area may find that the programs to be administered are involved in several departments separately and that serious investigation of the work involved in carrying out the legislation would involve work with several departments. This is simply*

too time-consuming and too complex to be undertaken without massive amounts of time and energy, and this is more than the committee staff generally has available, so oversight is not performed.

The visibility of the issue is a third aspect of subject matter relevant to oversight. Few congressmen can resist an opportunity for promoting their careers. Hence, the greater the likelihood of increased political visibility from a particular exercise of oversight, the more probable it is that oversight will be undertaken. A few members of the Congress are noted both for their impact on policy and for their anonymity, but most congressmen follow strategies that will enhance their visibility to the public.

Few issues are highly visible to most citizens. Congressmen think rather of their visibility to groups that are important to them. Which issues meet that test is related to the nature of each constituency, personal values, and career aspirations.

Committee Structure

A fourth opportunity factor is that of committee structure. Is the committee centralized or decentralized? How much latitude does the chairman permit or how much is he forced to accept? A highly centralized committee is unlikely to conduct much oversight without the active approval of the chairman. A decentralized committee—one in which power over money, staff, and program is largely in the hands of subcommittee chairmen or others—enhances the opportunity for oversight simply because decision-making is dispersed.[15]

The importance of the congressional committee in oversight is simply that almost all oversight occurs there. The Congress as a whole does not oversee. Nor does the House or the Senate. The particular committee or subcommittee rather than the parent body provides the most useful focus for analysis.

Status on a Committee

A fifth opportunity factor is status on a particular committee. The higher the status of the member on a committee, the more opportunity he will have to influence oversight. Occasionally oversight flows from the efforts of junior members, but the normal correlate to oversight is high status, such as that of a committee or subcommittee chairman. The ability of a junior member to influence the conduct of oversight is tied to the preferences of his committee or subcommittee chairman.

The connections between status and opportunity pose no mystery. Access to staff illustrates the linkage. Committee chairmen, subcommittee chairmen, and ranking minority members usually have the greatest opportunity to tap staff services. In theory, the staff members work for the entire committee; in practice, the use of staff time is determined from the top.

Relations with the Executive Branch

Legislative concern with executive behavior rests on factors other than profound policy and constitutional differences. A sixth set of opportunity factors reflects this reality. As James Robinson points out, congressional attitudes about bureaucratic behavior relate to the satisfaction congressmen feel with their treatment by an executive unit.[16]

Congressional behavior is also tied to whether congressmen have confidence in key personnel of the relevant executive departments. An important factor in creating a desire for oversight is the regard, high or low, which key decision makers in the Congress have for top officials in an executive department. The actions of one executive official are grist for legislative action; the same deed in the hands of another, for legislative acquiescence or approval. Thus Allen Drury records in *A Senate Journal:*

> *March 4, 1945. Fred Vinson, one of the congress darlings and an able man in his own right, has been nomi-*

nated federal loan administrator to succeed Jesse
[Jones]. This is greeted with great approval in the
Senate, where Fred is a deservedly popular man. All talk
of separating the vast, fantastic and inexcusable powers
of the agency has of course automatically stopped with
the appointment of a fellow everybody likes. [17]

Or, as Richard Fenno notes:

*Perhaps the most consistent thread in subcommittee
decision making is the sampling they do for the purpose
of deciding whether or not to tender their confidence to
an agency. Given the fact that their information is im-
perfect and given their large zone of uncertainty about
what the agency "really" needs, committee members
must necessarily act on the basis of confidence, trust, or
faith in agency officials. What they want to know, above
all else, about an agency or administrator is "Can I believe what he tells me? Will he do what he says he will
do?" So, they sample for information that will determine the degree of confidence they should have in an
agency—by "sizing up" an administrator at the hearings,
by asking detailed and specific questions of witnesses to
see if they know their job, by checking agency performance against last year's promises, and committee direc-
tives. If subcommittee members are satisfied with the
results of their sampling, they will willingly take agency
statements as fact. If they are not, if the agency does
not pass the test, legislators will remain extraordinarily
suspicious. Confidence is the cumulative product, obviously, of countless interchanges, formal and informal,
between committee and agency personnel over extended
periods of time. [18]*

And, according to a Democratic member of the House:

*It isn't just the "Executive" that is involved; it is the
plan and its spokesman. If he inspires confidence even*

though he is of the opposition party you trust him and feel he is not slipping a knife between your ribs or destroying something you believe in, if you think he knows what he is talking about you cooperate with him. If you don't trust him or believe he doesn't know what he is doing you treat him with a contempt he has earned. I saw this happen to Roosevelt's executives when the Democrats had substantial majorities. He had weak executives and they couldn't carry a paper bag down the Hill.[19]

Party affiliation is a third aspect of executive-legislative relations relevant for oversight. A congressman of the president's political party is less likely to be concerned with oversight than a member of the opposition party.[20] In 1966, Representative Florence P. Dwyer (R.–New Jersey), ranking minority member of the House Government Operations Committee, sponsored a bill to set up a special oversight committee controlled by the minority party when the same political party controlled both houses of the Congress. She noted:

Although the authority of Congress to investigate the operations of the executive branch is clear and undisputed, existing procedures are demonstrably inadequate when the same party controls both branches of the government. It is unrealistic to expect the congressional members of a political party, regardless of the party, to subject executive branch officials of the same party to the kind of complete and searching scrutiny required for the proper exercise of congressional oversight activity.[21]

All legislative decisions are not party decisions. Yet, as David Truman has convincingly demonstrated, the fact that the parties are neither monolithic nor diametrically opposed on all major policy issues does not mean that party has little relevance in legislative decision-making.[22]

Member Priorities

Member priorities form a seventh opportunity factor. Each member is faced with a variety of obligations that are legitimate, important, and demanding of time and energy. In principle, he should be working hard at all of them. In fact, since he does not weigh them equally, he is unlikely to give them equal attention. He may attend to all of the areas that he is supposed to cover, but he probably will not handle all of them well. As one respected legislative assistant put it, "There is a mystique in the House of Representatives that representatives must do everything. The reality of the matter is that representatives simply can't do it. Members are caught up in this mystique themselves. This gives them the feeling that they should be doing all of these things and they talk as if they are, whereas in fact, they really can't."

In making his choices about what to do, each congressman applies his own standards of relevance. Some things count for more than other things. Problems seen as less pressing may be recognized but may remain untouched. In these calculations, oversight frequently falls into the semi-neglected category. Choice, not accident, governs this decision.

The crucial question is with what skill and to what subject areas the congressman will devote his major energies. In principle, a congressman is always busy; in practice, the way he responds to intrusions and pressures defines his working life. In the words of Representative William Green (D.– Pennsylvania), "Each member is busy with day-to-day activities. No member has time to look out for problems or to try and create problems. We are always busy, but we can do more if we have to. The schedule is flexible, and if sensitive problems impinge on the member, the member can handle them, but he does not start a systematic search to look for problems." Representative Richard Bolling (D.–Missouri) argues similarly that congressmen are pretty much free to organize their time as they wish.[23] Contemplation of what he ought to do in a pressure-free context seldom molds his daily routine.

All members of the Congress are involved in a myriad of activities. The pressures for action are often substantial. The excuses for inaction can be equally impressive. In truth, a congressman may simply lack interest in many aspects of governmental activity. He is unlikely to generate much oversight activity in such subject areas. But even where his concern is clear, choices still have to be made in the context of a shortage of time, energy, and other resources such as his status on a committee or subcommittee. The higher the priority the congressman gives to an area of bureaucratic activity, the greater the possibility that he will engage in oversight in that policy area. As Seymour Scher convincingly points out, the primary calculus is that of gains and losses to the congressman. In such a calculus, oversight often has fewer potential payoffs than other activities.[24] According to an unusually knowledgeable staff member:

> *Members become concerned with the abstract obligation to oversee largely as they feel they can make a political record or on occasions where they differ in policy orientation from the bureaucrats involved.*
>
> *The apparent abstract concern with oversight as a function of the Congress is usually only a device to gloss over personal or policy differences or the desire to build a record.*

The major attention of the congressman will tend to be elsewhere. How much oversight captures his concern relates to its contribution to his political career. In the words of a sophisticated staff assistant to a senator, "Specialists in departmental interference must judge both the merits of the case and the costs in time, effort, in their own or the congressman's 'credit' with the agency, of attempting to achieve a given solution."[25]

As one study of the Senate Banking and Currency Committee concluded:

Senior members of Banking and Currency, those in the best position to make the committee active in oversight, often yield to alternative demands on their time. . . . Non—banking and currency responsibility, in conjunction with the lack of compelling interest in committee business on the part of the senior members, have restricted the committee as an oversight unit. [26]

An examination of each of these seven opportunity factors leads to the creation of hypotheses about the conduct of oversight. No single hypothesis, however, provides a sufficiently comprehensive explanation of the conditions under which the likelihood for oversight is advanced or retarded. There seems to be no single pattern which explains legislative oversight in all circumstances. There are only common factors which combine in different ways under specified sets of circumstances.

Preliminary analysis of these opportunity factors does yield an oversight-maximizing syndrome. Oversight is most likely to occur when the following are present: a legal basis for committee or individual activity, and money available; adequate staff resources defined in terms of numbers, skill, and attitudes; subject matter that is not unusually technical or complex enough to require special expertise; activities involved that are centralized in one executive department; an issue with high visibility and large political payoffs; decentralized committee operations or a chairman of the full committee who is a strong advocate of oversight in a given area; a desire of important people, usually those with committee or subcommittee chairmanships, to oversee; unhappiness of key committee members with the conduct of executive personnel, a lack of confidence in top executive personnel, or personal antipathy toward them; control of the house of the Congress involved by one political party and of the presidency by the other; poor treatment of members of the Congress, especially those on relevant committees, by executive officials; a member's strong interest in the work of his committee and the particular subject matter at hand; and committee positions highly sought by persons with more than average competence. In general, a minimizing syndrome is obtained by reversing these factors.

But what if these factors produce mixed results or indicate a high proclivity toward oversight? Does this mean that comprehensive and systematic oversight automatically results? Not necessarily. What, then, turns proclivity into behavior? Conversion factors help explain this.

Conversion Factors

Conversion factors define the most common situations in which propensities are converted into behavior. They seem to account most directly and immediately for specific oversight efforts.

What leads legislators to convert their opportunities into actual behavior? Sharp disagreement by congressmen with a new executive policy or with a substantial change in an existing policy provides strong stimuli to oversight even on subjects where scrutiny was modest previously. The more the legislator agrees with the program being implemented, the less likely he is to want to oversee; policy disagreement is a major stimulus to oversight.[27]

The most unpredictable of conversion factors is the impact of external events. A sudden crisis may stimulate attempts at oversight. A genuine scandal, or the appearance of one, may provide a stimulus sufficient to goad a congressman or a committee into action. A report by a constituent of how an agency treated him outrageously may promote congressional interest. Attention by a congressman is especially likely when the protestors are significant organized groups or constituents important to the congressman, or are supported by persons whom he respects or fears.

The impact of an external event may override legislative routines. Several pieces of legislation passed in the 1960s can be related to particular events, such as the assassinations of Senator Robert Kennedy and Martin Luther King, Jr. Just as a traumatic event can rescue stalled legislation, so can it lead to oversight efforts.

Crisis does not guarantee congressional action. No massive congressional investigation followed on the heels of the total collapse of postal service in Chicago in October 1966. In retrospect, though, the incident did precipitate pressure for reform from the executive branch which was later reflected in Congress. Congressional attention does not automatically follow any spectacular incident, but the presence of such an incident tends to convert predispositions into behavior. To paraphrase a well-worn saying, the Congress in crisis may well be the Congress at work. Still, policy by paroxysm is not the norm.

What This Study Does

To discover how opportunity and conversion factors interrelate and develop requires massive research into many situations over the years. If, as Richard F. Fenno, Jr., so pursuasively suggests, committees differ in their member goals and in their environmental constraints, then one could anticipate that their oversight behavior would vary as well. This is a reasonable hypothesis. At present, no one knows with certainty that it is true, and in the immediate future, no one is likely to find out. To seek out and fully elaborate whatever patterns exist is not feasible at this point.[28] The scope of the studies undertaken in this book is more modest. The intent is to apply the scheme of analysis presented herein to three committees and subcommittees in the United States House of Representatives over a period of some three years. In addition, some relationships between formal and latent oversight are probed.

The rationale for the particular cases studied requires some explanation. The bulk of the book deals with committee oversight behavior. But why these particular committees and subcommittees? In each instance, the criteria for selection were somewhat different. The House Post Office and Civil Service Committee was selected for study on the assumption that its low status in the House of Representatives would have important consequences for its oversight activities. Low-status committees are characterized by conscripted members, many of whom transfer from the committee as quickly as possible. How does this movement affect their behavior?

Most of the jurisdiction of the Post Office and Civil Service Committee covers technical, complex, and in the eyes of the general public, mundane matters. Gaining expertise in these matters provides no easy road to political visibility. Yet the Post Office Department carries out many routine activities seemingly typical of what the government does. How do these facts about subject matter relate to oversight activity?

Finally, a powerful set of interest groups played a decisive role in the functioning of the Post Office and Civil Service Committee both on matters of legislation and on oversight. In what ways did this relationship shape committee behavior?

The House Judiciary Committee, and particularly its Subcommittee Five, provides a comparison and at the same time a sharp contrast. Membership on the Judiciary Committee was sought. Most of its members did want to be there. The membership of Subcommittee Five was a hand-picked group with strong interests in civil rights questions. Civil rights policy was immensely complicated politically, but the rewards of mastering these intricacies were substantial both in personal publicity and in having an impact on a central public policy question. The issues before Subcommittee Five were the same ones flashing across newspaper headlines almost daily. Interest-group pressures were surely exerted not only in the name of immediate gain for individual members but on behalf of broader constituencies concerned with national policy questions.

Unlike the Post Office and Civil Service Committee, Judiciary Subcommittee Five scored high on opportunity factors; yet like the Post Office Committee in the period under study, it apparently conducted little oversight. Did appearance match reality or was oversight being performed in less than obvious ways, perhaps latently? Subcommittee Five was highly active in considering civil rights legislation yet apparently was not much involved in oversight. This seeming paradox requires discussion and explanation.

The House Government Operations Committee, particularly its Special Subcommittee on the Invasion of Privacy, is a third subject for study. The status of the special subcommittee was always insecure. Its history was short. The staff was small. There were only three members on the subcommittee; and their major priorities were elsewhere. The issues involved were highly volatile at the time of consideration but involved endless routine afterward. The subcommittee was essentially homogeneous in its policy orientation toward questions concerning invasion of privacy and was unanimously hard-working. The impact of this subcommittee was initially very sharp in achieving its desired oversight results, essentially without the use of legislation. Why was this subcommittee, so low in opportunity factors, so active in oversight behavior? Why, in the face of such frequent frustration flowing from the factors listed above, could this subcommittee accomplish a great deal in the area of oversight?

These studies of committee-bureaucracy interaction composing chapters 2 through 5 are designed to relate examples of congressional oversight behavior to their relevant conditioning factors. There is no intention to assert that these same committees and subcommittees will behave the same way at all times. On the contrary, following the scheme of analysis outlined leads to the conclusion that the same groups will act differently if the factors described change their complexion. The point is that the scheme of analysis presented here will be able to shed light on this altered behavior. In the early 1970s, both the Post Office and the Judiciary committees were behaving somewhat differently in their oversight efforts, but these changes could be explained handily by the same scheme of analysis used in these chapters. The Special Subcommittee on the Invasion of Privacy is now defunct.

Chapter 6 deals essentially with some formal techniques for oversight, but from a functional perspective. Oversight as a latent function, neither recognized nor necessarily intended, is emphasized. The intent is to discuss the use of three formal techniques, the circumstances that accompany their use, and the results achieved or not achieved. Specifically considered will be certain relationships between casework and oversight, and the use of legislative hearings and required reports as oversight devices.

In all, these elaborate probings into a variety of institutional settings, processes, and behavior are designed to produce more data about oversight than are presently available and provide an analysis of them. This expansion and development of existing research should provide some useful insights into the conduct of oversight in the Congress as well as establish a useful base for further research.

How the Congress oversees the federal bureaucracy may not determine whether the American political system will survive. Congressional involvement surely does shape much public policy; congressional activity also affects which issues will never reach the governmental agenda. A process which has these potential impacts deserves attention.

Chapter 2 The House Post Office and Civil Service Committee

In the 89th Congress, the House Post Office and Civil Service Committee was housed in a string of bleak offices on the third floor of the Cannon House Office Building. The atmosphere was one of pervasive calm and routine work. There was no air of electricity here. The office of the chairman, strategically situated next to the committee hearing room, was open intermittently. A sense of calm and gloom governed the air. Absent were the scurrying secretaries, the staccato of electric typewriters, the earnest staff assistants moving in and out. There were few movements to and from the office of the chairman.[1] A secretary stopping to gossip with a friend might have been characteristic. The hearing room, only occasionally used, was seldom filled with spectators; the dais was rarely occupied by a full quota of members. What went on was sometimes relevant, occasionally aimless, but seldom the stuff that attracts newsmen or large crowds. The sense of anticipation lurking around the fringes of a potentially explosive hearing was rarely found.

Only on a few occasions did the atmosphere alter and then usually because the committee seemed poised for a decision on a federal employees pay bill. Lobbyists then crowded the corridor near the massive, closed, double doors. Like the old friends they were, they gossiped and joked, passing the time before the day's moment of truth—a decision on a pay bill—was reached. The scene was reminiscent of a small-town railroad station where people congregated to await the day's major event—the coming of the train.

27

Less apparent was the endless telephoning, the drafting of documents, the quiet consulting, and the reading of reports, which defined the routine of committee work. On the surface, not much was happening. What was really going on? And was it any different from the placid atmosphere? If the congress in committee is the congress at work, what was the work here, how was it being accomplished, and why was this the case? For purposes of this study, only the oversight activities of the committee are being considered.

The oversight activities of the Post Office and Civil Service Committee can be analyzed through a discussion of the opportunity and conversion factors listed in chapter 1. The opportunity factors taken together provide an index of a committee's predisposition to oversee.

Legal Powers

The first of these factors is that of formal-legal powers. The Post Office and Civil Service Committee shares the characteristics common to all standing committees. Like other committees, the House Post Office and Civil Service Committee is assigned a jurisdiction for special concern. In 1965, this jurisdiction extended to census and collection of statistics generally; federal civil service generally; national archives; postal savings banks; postal service generally; and the status of officers and employees of the United States. The jurisdiction of any committee, however minor, can challenge the interests of its members. While its work may be pale in interest when compared to the Rules Committee or the Ways and Means Committee, even the Post Office and Civil Service Committee confronts problems that are substantial and complex.

A committee's jurisdiction places boundaries on what the committee will do; it does not determine in which of its assigned areas the committee will act. Its jurisdiction shapes which executive department will ask it for legislation, which administrative units it will investigate, and with which executive personnel the committee members and staff will most frequently interact. A congressional committee is not normally a freely roaming body in search of an issue.

Committee jurisdiction does provide a ready rationalization in support of whatever specific actions are undertaken. The formal-legal powers of the committee shape the areas within which the committee acts, but primarily in providing a routine focus for committee operations. In this sense, formal-legal powers provide an opportunity which committee members can choose to exploit or ignore.

All committees also share the mandate of the Legislative Reorganization Act of 1946:

> *Each standing committee of the Senate and the House of Representatives shall exercise continuous watchfulness of the execution by the administrative agencies concerned, of any laws, the subject matter of which is within the jurisdiction of such committees.*[2]

Staff Resources

Staff resources constitute a second opportunity factor. The committee staff itself seldom determines its own behavior. The staff normally reflects the attitudes and preferences of committee leaders, partly because staff members are frequently appointed through the influence of these leaders. The Post Office Committee is no exception: The committee counsel was the nominee of a senior Democrat on the committee, and the assistant staff director served for many years in the office of the ranking minority member of the committee before moving over to the committee staff.

Logic does not demand that a master-servant relationship follow. But staff members know how they are appointed and are aware of the obligation involved. In fact, one ranking committee Democrat sends his committee work and some of his work from his district to "his staff man." With rare exceptions, the basic factor in explaining staff behavior is the desires and behavior of the members. When the relationship is somewhat different, that situation is widely recognized. Thus, the staff director for the Manpower Subcommittee was known in the Congress and "Downtown" for his aggressiveness and initiative in investigations. One staff member commented: "Most of the work of the subcommittee is staff-initiated." Another added, "On the Manpower Subcommittee, the basic source of most legislative oversight is the staff itself. The committee is well staffed and does extensive work in the oversight area." The chairman of the subcommittee confirmed this: "The staff provides most of the ideas for studies." A leading member of the White House staff whose work involved extensive relationships with the Post Office Committee noted:

> *Occasionally, oversight is promoted by the presence of an aggressive staff member, although this is not too common. The leading example is the Manpower Subcommittee of the House Post Office and Civil Service Committee, where Bun Bray is very active and articulate and has translated his efforts into hearings in many cases.*

Even in the presence of unusual staff energy and talent, cooperation from the chairman remains basic to continued success.

By all accounts, the core professional staff of the Post Office and Civil Service Committee exhibits skill, diligence, and technical competence. Almost all members of the committee, junior and senior, Republican and Democrat, respect the competence and fairness of the staff. "The staff is adequate and provides me with all the information services that I request." "The committee staff is okay. It is nonpartisan. It works for me as well as for anyone else." Even a Republican member who had little respect for many of his colleagues noted: "I have a good deal of respect for the staff. I trust the staff. They will perform effectively for me." Another minority member reported: "The staff is very useful. It is competent and unusually nonpartisan." "I trust the staff. I consult the minority staff members only if there are clear party policy questions involved. I do not choose between them otherwise." "The committee staff is a good one." "The committee staff is considerably better than that of many other committees. I can use the staff. They always have the ability to do what I ask them to do."

The staff director had long experience in government, in both the executive and legislative branches. The associate director was almost equally experienced, having served "seventeen years on the executive side." The staff counsel was competent and diligent. The assistant staff director had long experience in postal matters.

Outside this hard core were a number of intermediate-level professional persons, usually assigned to particular subcommittees and selected by the subcommittee chairman. A large number of clerical employees appointed through the influence of several sources, including the Speaker of the House, completed the staff.

The committee staff provided the basis, in numbers, for extensive oversight of bureaucratic activity. The technical competence was there. But here again, what seemed crucial was not technical competence and numbers, but staff attitudes about oversight essentially as derived from member attitudes. In the words of one staff member with an analytical bent:

> *There is no one on the staff who is aggressively concerned with oversight. Many staff members are technically competent. The senior people work hard, but their orientation is essentially toward serving the member's immediate needs. They are more interested in preserving the status quo than in seriously inquiring into the activities of the bureaucracy.*

A minority view came from a former top staff member, perhaps reflecting his previous role. "The staff is the basic element in oversight. Its size, its quality, and its energy are important elements in explaining what oversight shall be done." What is perhaps confused here is what is necessary and what is sufficient.

Most committee members thought that the size of the staff was adequate for committee needs. They did not see a correlation between increasing staff size and more significant oversight. One person intimately involved with the Congress on personnel matters went further: "More staff might result in more trivia being dealt with." One interesting sidelight is that the very few members who did advocate staff increases were highly active on other committees and found it difficult to serve effectively on the Post Office and Civil Service Committee, for them a second priority.

The relevance of staff size is related also to the ability of lobbyists to perform functions that might normally be handled by the formal staff. It is relatively common in the Congress to find interest groups performing substantial tasks of research and reporting for members. In 1967, one newspaper reported:

> Mr. Kerlin [Don Kerlin, lobbyist for several interest groups] was the subject of a controversy last week when he reportedly attended a closed-door session of the Postal Rates Subcommittee, headed by Rep. Arnold Olsen, Montana Democrat. Members of the subcommittee denied the reports and the full committee passed a resolution saying that it hadn't happened.
>
> But Mr. Olsen conceded that Mr. Kerlin may have been consulted as a "technician" on the rate bill approved by his subcommittee.[3]

In the case of the House Post Office and Civil Service Committee, as will be shown later, interest groups performed major staff functions.

Many members saw a more direct relationship between better staff *quality* and improved oversight. This view was shared by top officials in the bureaucracy and among senior committee members themselves. One astute observer who has traveled the paths of executive office, committee staff member, and consultant in both Republican and Democratic administrations, argued: "The critical staff question is its quality." An equally experienced participant added: "The problem is not really more people, but more top-rate people. People who are experienced and able enough to handle the kinds of work that a good staff is required to do are very scarce. It's not a question of having more money but availability of people."

Subject Matter

A third opportunity factor is the subject matter under discussion. The likelihood of oversight is enhanced if the subject matter is not so technical and complex that considerable time and talent are required to master it; if a substantive area is handled in a single department or agency; and if the issue is highly visible to individuals and groups perceived by the members as being politically relevant.

The more complex and technical the subject matter, the more time members and staff must provide if oversight is to be undertaken. A high-ranking official in the Post Office Department with much experience on the Hill captured the essence of the situation in discussing the problems that arose in instituting the zip code system:

> *Congress cannot really win such battles because they are not willing to pay the price. The price is continuing day-to-day attention and concern. Congressmen cannot be interested, and are not interested, in these day-to-day routine things. Congressmen tend to be interested only in the spectacular situations.*

Few subjects are so complex as to preclude congressional mastery, but the investment sometimes must be high. Committees in the Congress, if they chose to devote sufficient resources to many problems in the bureaucracy, could get at and stay on top of them. A deficiency in oversight may lie less in the availability of resources than in their allocation.

Most members of the Congress could, with enough time and energy, master many subjects. As will be demonstrated in chapter 3, member priorities on this committee made it unlikely that such expertise would develop. For many, the incentives to oversee were not sufficient to warrant investing the time, energy, and other resources required. One consequence was a tendency to focus on discrete, narrowly focused issues which could be studied with modest investment. A second tendency was to focus on dramatic issues with high emotional quotients; such issues did not necessarily involve fundamental questions. Thus, studies of the work measurement program in the Post Office devoted much attention to the use of stopwatches in clocking the speed of some postal workers. The Post Office Department viewed this congressional concern as trivial:

> *Congressmen tend to deal with details and trivia partly because they feel incapable of dealing with the great big problems, some of which simply have no solutions and which can be managed at best only after extensive and exhaustive work requiring much time and energy. They attempt to deal with details in terms of something they actually can measure.*

Representative Albert Johnson (R.–Pennsylvania) pointed out some of these problems in discussing his work on his other committee, Banking and Currency. Representative Johnson had extensive experience in banking before coming to the Congress. Yet, "many of the problems I have to deal with were unusual and beyond my experience." Since few members of the House Post Office Committee have had extensive experience in postal affairs before coming to the Congress, the problem was even more acute for them.

How one perceives this fundamental problem of priorities and competence is related to one's perspectives. The committee counsel noted that "most of the items that come through the committee are relatively simple. If they required much preparation, they would create difficulties because the members are so busy. They would find it difficult to prepare in such cases."

One interest-group spokesman who was highly critical of the committee and its work interpreted the same data with a harsher twist:

It is lucky that most of the work before the Post Office Committee is simple because most of the members simply don't understand it. There are few people on the committee that understand the overall issues. This is evidenced by the quality of the questions they raise in public as well as by their private activities.

The operation of the committee has to depend essentially on the work of a few people who are bright enough to understand the really complicated problems that occur. The rest take their cues from them, the administration, or from the employee groups as the case may be.

Most members of the committee suggested that the committee handled the major issues reasonably well but slighted some less crucial areas. The possible points of contention about these contrasting conclusions include that of identifying the major issues. Interviews with the members and staff revealed that they perceived these issues to be the annual pay bill and the postal rates bills.

The committee spent considerable time on topics seemingly far removed from those central to running an effective Post Office. A glance at these may reveal something about the problems of oversight on this committee. In the time interval studied, two such issues stood out: obscenity in the mails and propaganda in the mail from Communist countries. If there was dispute over the importance of these issues, there was agreement that their emotional content and publicity value were high.

A senior staff member cited the problem of obscenity in the mails as one of the two major committee efforts at oversight in recent years. Extensive hearings were held in 1959, and others were held in 1960, 1962, 1964, and 1965. Commenting on these, a highly placed official in the Post Office Department asserted:

> *Typical of the congressional lack of concern for the basic problems in the department is the obscenity issue, which has received great publicity over the years. This is an easy, gut political issue; the time and effort spent there illustrate the basic lack of concern in the Congress with the basic issues.*

In discussing the obscenity issue, another highly placed official in the Post Office Department added: "Those damn bills! The obscenity bills are largely a matter of going on the record to please some constituents. This is an attempt to simplify a complex problem in terms his constituents can understand."

Implicit is a judgment not only about relative priorities in the Congress but also about the public relations aspect of oversight activities. What is ignored, of course, are the representative and educational functions of the member of Congress. But even senior committee staff members suggested that perhaps the committee made more of the obscenity issue than it deserved. Part of the motivation was surely publicity. Perhaps involved as well was a tendency for some members to devote vast amounts of time and resources that only could be found by ignoring fundamental problems. Others gain a reputation that way.

Illustrating the same point was the committee's concern

with the problem of censorship of mail from Communist countries. The value of such censorship can be disputed, but it was surely remote from the basic problems facing a post office hovering on the brink of disaster. Again, from the focus of highly placed Post Office Department officials:

> *The problems involved in receiving and registering this material are massive. Running this program of sending out requests to persons and filing of cards requesting materials costs the Post Office a great deal of money, but congressmen find that they can pound their chests on this and make a lot of noise and go ahead and do it. So at the same time as they cut budget and call for economy they put through programs like this which create a great deal of difficulty in the Post Office Department and aren't really worth a damn.*

These examples suggest a hypothesis: the greater the drama and visibility of an issue to individuals and groups perceived as politically relevant by congressional decision makers, the more likely it is that oversight will occur.

Normally not much publicity comes to members of the House Post Office and Civil Service Committee because, as one member puts it, "This committee deals normally with low-key issues." Another member lamented: "I don't know why anyone would want to study this committee, it's so dull." The staff director confirmed these judgments: "Most of the work of this committee is relatively obscure." Normally, the publicity value of work on the committee is low, so "congressmen tend to be interested in spectacular situations, the situations where there is great publicity, for example, where big robberies occur or where there is some sensational snafu in service."

A senior official in the Post Office Department summarized succinctly: "Where there is publicity to be gained, there is oversight to be had." A lobbyist suggested:

> *Congress oversees the executive when there is a dramatic issue or a very visible hardship. Given the organization of the Congress and given their dependence upon the administration, given their long-established ways of doing things, it is very difficult for the Congress to change.*

Despite the value of publicity, very few issues of policy capture the attention of the entire public. A more relevant focus is the publics perceived as politically relevant. For this committee, in many instances, the relevant target was a small number of interest groups. This thesis will be developed in chapter 3.

Committee Structure and Procedures

A fourth opportunity factor is committee structure and procedures. The most relevant of these is whether the committee is centralized or decentralized in its operations.

The correlation between centralization and increased or decreased oversight is seldom direct. A centralized committee is one whose activities are closely bound to the preferences and priorities of the chairman or whoever possesses de facto political power on the committee. If the chairman is an avid overseer, then centralization leads to substantial oversight; if the chairman resists oversight, on a centralized committee, the probability of oversight activity drops sharply.

On a decentralized committee, arithmetic takes over. The chances of finding subcommittee chairmen who are eager to oversee are greater simply because if more people have political power, some of them may want to use it. In the absence of other knowledge about a committee, one would assume that a decentralized committee structure provides greater opportunity for oversight activity.

The experience of the House Post Office and Civil Service Committee fortifies these conclusions. Before 1965, it was essentially a centralized, chairman-dominated committee. After its reorganization, called by some the Revolution of 1965, the committee became much more decentralized. What impact did this change have on the conduct of oversight?

The chairman of the committee, Tom Murray (D.–Tennessee), was frequently cited as an administration spokesman. Some argued that not much oversight was done because the chairman wished it that way. A close and friendly colleague was more sympathetic: "Mr. Murray has always felt that an investigation should never be made unless there is a strong case for it." This attitude of the chairman, complemented by his increasing infirmity, determined committee behavior. One close associate noted generously, "In recent years, the chairman has been a sick and elderly man and has not been as active as he once was." Critics of the chairman explained committee inactivity somewhat differently.

One reason for the committee reorganization in 1965 was that some members wanted a more active and vital committee. Most of the interviewing for this study was done in 1965 and 1966, shortly after the reorganization and perhaps too soon after the event to detect whether a new pattern of committee behavior had emerged. Each observer tended to view the motivations of the "revolutionaries" somewhat differently, but at least one motive was the desire for action from a somnolent committee. On the whole, persons on and around the committee saw the reorganization as leading to more activity, but not necessarily to activity of a higher quality.

Those who felt that the committee was not working more effectively than before tended to focus on the power and publicity aspects of the structural changes. "What the changes accomplished was basically to allow more members to get more publicity and to get into the newspapers more often, and that is really what they want." Another close observer of the committee added, "Previously, Murray had made all the decisions. Now it was possible for the members themselves, as chairmen of the subcommittees, to gain power and to gain publicity." A member of the committee who opposed the reorganization but who did want more activity from the committee concluded: "There was personal aggrandizement on the part of the members involved. Those who were responsible will invent high-sounding phrases for what they did."

Most members did think that improved oversight had taken place since the "revolution" but that the change could have come in other ways. The links between personal promotion and willingness to oversee can be close. A minority of interviewees viewed the reorganization simply as a power grab. As one member of the committee put it, "Although I favored the committee reorganization in 1965, I did so more because the reorganization provided more power to the subcommittee chairmen than for reasons of ideological differences with the full committee chairman." One Post Office official, closely involved in dealing with the committee and a self-styled pragmatist, felt that:

> *Power used to be centralized in the committee, and the executive dealing with the Congress could take account of that fact of life. Now the subcommittee chairmen have autonomy so that what was previously cleared with the chairman would now be cleared, perhaps, with the subcommittee chairmen. Subcommittee chairmen gained power that they hadn't had before. They want to exercise this power and do so for their own advantage. This means more extensive consultation for us.*

Whatever the roots of the revolution, most members, staff people, and close observers from the executive branch saw more oversight activity emerging after the change. "Since the reorganization, the committee participated in more detail than it ever had before." An assistant secretary in the Post Office Department made a judgment shared by other high-ranking officials in the department: "The committee has become more active but this creates problems for the department in the sense that more testimony is needed than we needed previously; more of our time has to be spent preparing the testimony as well as giving it." One junior member of the committee summed up the majority sentiment:

> *I didn't choose the committee; I was assigned to it. I might well stay on this committee. This is partly because of the reorganization which took place in 1965 where the subcommittees were given more autonomy, in which it was made possible for the committee to be more active. This reorganization had an impact on legislative activity and on oversight. More oversight can be done effectively now.*

Taken together, these comments focus on the potential for more activity. Structure may not directly cause activity, but structural changes can increase the opportunity for oversight.

Status on a Committee

The fifth opportunity factor is one's status on a committee. The opportunity for oversight is promoted if one is a committee chairman, subcommittee chairman, or sometimes a ranking minority member of a committee or subcommittee. The junior member with a sharp impact on committee proceedings is sufficiently rare to require notice. One junior member articulated political reality: "There is more democracy in the operation of my subcommittees than I ever expected." Another freshman noted, "Although I do not brag about it too much, I feel I have gained a modest measure of influence on the subcommittee where I am a ranking member." Two facts stand out: the chairman is not omnipotent; the freshmen are rather surprised when they can shape events.

The impact of junior members is modest even for those

few who make this committee a top priority and who gain the respect of their colleagues. Such a person was Representative Paul Krebs (D.–New Jersey), who because of traditions in his district and because of his own labor union background actually sought membership on this committee and devoted his major attention to its work. Still, he said, "I have not put forth any suggestions for major studies or investigations. I feel it is presumptuous for a freshman to undertake such activity. I do have access to the subcommittee chairman. I have had several minor things which have been expeditiously handled in this regard."

The importance of this testimony is twofold: it suggests the interaction basis for political leadership, even when freshmen are involved; and second, given the large turnover on this committee, a distinct faction of the membership usually consists of members new to the Congress.

Interviewees repeatedly stated that the chairman of a subcommittee made the basic decisions for the subcommittee. The ranking minority member was generally consulted by the chairman. How much he was consulted was a function of the chairman's style and of the need for minority votes. Committee members agreed that the closer the party margin on a committee, the more likely it was that consultation would occur. If the votes of the minority were needed, they would be consulted. Other members of a subcommittee felt free to bring their ideas to the chairman; some chairmen were even quite receptive to suggestions. But ultimately, short of a rare revolutionary situation, the position of the chairman prevailed. In the words of a junior committee member: "Other members are free to bring things to the chairman. They will be given a receptive ear, but basically it is the staff and the chairman who run the committees and the subcommittees."

One chairman of a subcommittee expressed the sentiment of the others: "I run my subcommittee with full consultation." The basis for effective leadership is the combination of formal resources and personal political skill. In the words of a veteran staff member:

> *Money is the key. The chairman controls the funds for the work of the committee. The chairman controls the appointment of the staff. The chairman has power over who is called to testify. He is the one who attends the meetings with House administration leaders. So the chairman's role is really a crucial one.*

The consultative process was captured by a majority member: "The minority members of a committee may have some voice, but they find it difficult to act since the chairman really controls things." Consultation can really mean ratification: "Sometimes I call my subcommittee together to present a series of routine actions that I have taken. They will just automatically approve of them." One subcommittee chairman described his consultation process: "I usually select the areas of emphasis for my subcommittee. I listen to all viewpoints. Sometimes differences in ideology mean the minority will be ignored. I am willing to respect minority suggestions when they are good ones." When asked how often the minority had good ideas, he smiled and said: "Well, they sometimes do. I do try and provide an opportunity for all those involved to have a say at least."

The chairman of the subcommittee will normally dominate the day-to-day activities of his committee. He will listen to ideas from others, but he is unlikely to accept them unless they fit somewhere into a frame of reference relevant and attractive for him. On the Post Office and Civil Service Committee, the interrelationships of structure and status were clear. As a result of the reorganization of 1965, which in many ways effectively decentralized the committee, power was dispersed, but mainly to the subcommittee chairmen rather than to the committee as a whole. The reorganization should be seen as a case study in the circulation of elites rather than as a revolt of the masses.

Quite revealing, then, were the results of a two-and-a-half-hour interview with Congressman James Morrison (D.–Louisiana), a subcommittee chairman and de facto committee chairman.[4] Whatever question was asked, the responses quickly turned to a discussion of interest groups as they affected the committee, casework as it stimulated committee activity, and attitudes about the personalities and competence of top Post Office Department officials. It is no coincidence that each of these factors loomed large in an analysis of committee activity.

Relations with the Executive

A sixth set of opportunity factors which condition oversight can be subsumed under the heading of member relations with the executive. These relationships will be considered under three subheadings: satisfaction with treatment by the agency concerned, regard for top executive officials, and partisan control of the executive and legislative branches.

Satisfaction with Treatment by the Agency Concerned

James Robinson, in *Congress and Foreign Policy-Making*, noted the difficulties in relating congressional satisfaction with treatment by an agency and voting on policy questions.[5] The information gathered in this study does not dissolve the complexity of these relationships. Most members of the Post Office Committee hesitated to discuss themselves or their colleagues in this regard; the senior officials in the Post Office Department, committee staff members, and lobbyists felt bound by no such inhibitions. These observers saw a strong connection between congressional unwillingness to oversee the Post Office Department actively and departmental treatment of congressmen. As will be demonstrated shortly, an abstinence-favors relationship is not adequate for explanatory purposes, yet these two factors do seem related.

At issue are not sordid tales of bribes, graft, and intrigue, but rather a more mundane set of benefits that the Post Office Department provided for members of the Congress. One of these was simple personal attention to the requests and problems of congressmen. When Lawrence O'Brien was postmaster general, the younger members of the committee were singled out for special attention. O'Brien assumed accurately that the senior members of the committee had already developed preferences and sources of information and therefore needed less routine attention than the newer members. So, quietly and regularly, the liaison men from the department visited the freshman congressmen and tried to tend to their questions and needs. This venture carried across party lines yet was sufficiently unobtrusive that a senior Republican member of the committee was surprised that his younger Republican colleagues were receiving this attention. Changes in voting behavior as a result of this solicitous attitude were not to be expected, but the building of good will had one clear result. As one very conservative Republican suggested:

> *There is always the possibility, of course, that O'Brien is pulling a snow job on me as well as on the others, but I do not think so. He seems genuinely interested in getting congressional viewpoints, and involving them in the process of policy-making for the Post Office Department, and in running it more satisfactorily. I feel that he is doing an excellent job in trying to reorganize the Post Office Department.*

One episode illustrated the thoroughness of the O'Brien method. One young member of the committee, who was a close personal friend of O'Brien's and who for personal, ideological, and party reasons was very likely to go along with O'Brien's policy requests, still found himself the regular object of departmental liaison visits. Busy on other questions where his decisions were more in doubt, he sometimes "threw them out," saying, "Don't worry about me. Go spend your time elsewhere." "In my case," he adds, "they are too solicitous. They are probably more effective when they administer this treatment elsewhere."

Younger committee members know that they lack easy opportunities to promote oversight. The O'Brien formula for building good will probably minimizes further any sentiment toward seeking systematic oversight. Good will and decision-making behavior are difficult to correlate directly; good will and the decision not to act can probably be more closely linked.

Cultivating members of the Post Office and Civil Service Committee is one concrete illustration of a philosophy O'Brien articulated more generally: "The human element is present, as it is in all activities in life, and the closer the relationship, the better the understanding, the greater the possibilities of ultimate enactment of the White House proposals."[6]

A second mundane benefit which the department provided to members of the Congress is publicity. One high-ranking official illustrated how the top-level staff in the Post Office Department promoted publicity for members:

> *O'Brien goes out regularly to dedicate post offices. We have the congressman come along with us. He has his picture taken with us. We issue statements and invite congressmen to add a paragraph to the statement. Congressmen seek power and publicity, and the department tries to make it possible for them to get both.*

The Post Office Department also provided adjustments in service for members in their districts. Items that never make the newspaper headlines are important to the person and groups involved. An assistant postmaster general noted: "They are trying to get along with us because we can do things for them. A businessman wants his mail delivered earlier in the day. Someone has to get their mail early. A properly presented plea by a congressman may get some results."

A veteran staff member deemphasized the most widely discussed form of favor, patronage in jobs:

Congress hesitates to oversee the Post Office more strictly not because of patronage questions regarding appointments. A series of smaller, less publicized things provide the answer. For example, getting a new post office in one's district, getting special consideration for large mailers in one's district, obtaining a new substation, extending door-to-door delivery rapidly into a new suburban area where there might be only curbside delivery otherwise.

Senior members of committees usually make most committee policy. Where key members of the committee were not inclined to oversee a department systematically, such action was not very likely. Hence, departments tend to be unusually solicitous of them. One key member of the committee was regarded by the Post Office Department as an unusually hard bargainer for his cooperation. According to a legislative liaison man, he "will do anything, but he has his price. I think that he saves things that he wants from the department on a list. When we call him to get help on programs, I almost feel as if he has a priority list ready so he can tell us what his help will cost in service returned."

These illustrations in no way demonstrate that diligence is directly decreased because of departmental favors to members of the Congress. Where the opportunity for oversight tends to be slight, it is probably made even more modest by a careful departmental program to promote satisfaction among members of the committee.

Regard for Top Executive Officials

Students of human behavior assert that one views the conduct of others partly through a lens formed by likes and dislikes for the persons involved. We try to reconcile the statements and actions of those whom we like personally with our own; we exaggerate the differences in statements and behavior between ourselves and those we personally dislike. This generalization probably holds for executive-legislative relations also. How members of the Congress, and especially members of the Post Office Committee, viewed top officials in the Post Office Department was relevant in explaining the probability of oversight.

This relationship is especially strong in a situation where technical expertise and full awareness of data may be lacking and hence where other indicators shape behavior. Since for many members of this committee, subject matter competence was nominal, factors such as interpersonal relationships became more important.

Three consequences of the presence of personal regard or lack of it for top executive officials can be hypothesized. The higher the congressional regard for the official, the better his treatment before congressional committees; second, the higher the congressional regard for top executive officials, the more likely that such officials can get their programs through the Congress; third, the higher the congressional regard for top executive officials, the less the likelihood of vigorous oversight.

The evidence in support of the first hypothesis is overwhelming. The committee treated Postmaster General Lawrence O'Brien with respect and even diffidence; Postmaster General John Gronouski was driven to anger by abusive questioning from the committee. One assistant postmaster general tried to explain this difference:

> *Gronouski was a fine man in his own way, but just over his head in this particular job, and as soon as Congress found that out, they began to let him have it. Some congressmen can't resist jumping on a man who can't defend himself adequately. O'Brien had great rapport, great political savvy, knew what made Congress run, worked hard at cooperation, and this makes a great deal of difference.*

A powerful committee member echoed these thoughts:

Gronouski was not a very effective postmaster, and the committee was very independent and could run rough-shod over him. The hearings on the zip code illustrate this. Gronouski didn't have what is needed for the job: talent, energy, and ambition. O'Brien, on the other hand, understands the committee and understands the Congress. He is willing to work and is more of a political man, willing to bargain things out.

A younger Democrat on the committee made a similar comparison:

Congress just didn't trust Gronouski under some situations. This was partly because Gronouski deceived Congress on a summer intern program and then tried to put the blame elsewhere. You can trust Larry O'Brien. If Congress trusts and respects the individual and thinks he is honest, if they think he is providing the best case possible, if his case seems to make some sense on the surface, congressmen will generally agree to it.

The links between high regard and policy promotion need to be carefully drawn. In some situations, high congressional regard for top executive officials pays off in legislative victories. Whether or not he is correct in the particular case, the following judgment of an assistant postmaster general is widely accepted on the Hill: "The parcel post bill could not have gone through in 1966 without Larry O'Brien as postmaster general." In situations where other pluses and minuses tend to balance out, congressional regard for executive sponsors of a program is highly relevant to victory or defeat.[7] But in situations where other factors are not so evenly balanced, such regard is an insufficient lever. The same assistant postmaster general added: "Not even O'Brien could get enough money to have six-day service restored in the Post Office where it had been cut out previously."

The evidence on the third hypothesis linking regard or lack of it for high executive officials with the presence or absence of vigorous congressional oversight is extensive and clear. A top official in the Post Office Department argued: "Because we are well liked in the Congress and sensitive to congressional needs, the pressure for oversight is relaxed. The congressmen know that O'Brien and I seek ways to keep them happy. This affects their attitude toward the department."

A minority member of the committee saw personality and personal relationships as basic:

> The personality of the postmaster general is basic in terms of explaining some aspects of oversight. If he at a given time seems bumbling and inefficient, this provides an opportunity for oversight that might not be present otherwise. Members of the Congress tend to give postmaster generals that they regard as ineffective a little extra hard time.

A staff member with extensive experience as a lobbyist summarized: "If they like the people, they will do less with oversight. If they are antagonized by those people, then congressmen will be more prone to oversight." One senior member of the committee, known as a keen analyst of the Congress, commented:

> One variable for explaining oversight is the respect that legislators have for individual administrators. Individuals that they like, that they respect, and that they have had mutually satisfactory relationships with, will have more discretion and get much less flack from congressmen than will those administrators that are not sensitive to the needs and desires of the Congress and to whom congressmen are somewhat antagonistic.

More briefly, a member stated: "Because the committee has confidence in O'Brien, it doesn't look as closely as to what is going on in the bureaucracy as it might." Thus the attitudes of congressmen toward the top-level bureaucrats increase or diminish in a variety of ways the opportunity for oversight.

Partisan Control of the Executive and Legislative Branches

Partisanship is a third dimension of congressional-executive relations that has consequences for oversight. In the absence of cohesive ideological political parties, party is not necessarily a determining factor in explaining congressional behavior toward the executive. More concrete evidence on this relationship is needed. On the Post Office and Civil Service Committee, members agreed that if the majority party was somewhat united and if its committee margin was substantial enough, then it could do what it wanted to. One of these conditions was present on the committee at the time of the interviews for this study. The Democrats held a large majority on the committee, 17—8. Because the Democrats were not always united, the analysis became more complex. The issue is not any abstract notion of the role of political parties, but the very concrete problem of majority-building for action. In the words of a veteran staff member and former Post Office Department official: "In most cases, the majority on the committee consults the minority only when the minority votes are needed or might be needed. Even today [1966], when the Democrats have a large majority on the committee, still the Republicans are needed on occasion, and when they are, they are consulted."

Two types of factors assist in thinking more precisely about how partisanship affects oversight. The first is the importance of the issue. The second factor is the level of behavior under discussion. The more important the issue the more likely the relevance of partisanship for committee behavior. On the minor day-to-day issues, most members and observers of the committee agreed that partisanship was minimal. As the issues became more prominent, the majority party tended to unite overtly for control.

> *Party lines are not of great importance on this commit-
> tee most of the time. Party becomes important when
> leaders outside the committee begin to put pressure on
> committee members. When the administration puts the*

screws on or when Dirksen or Ford puts pressures on
the Republicans, then party lines may well be drawn.

A minority member on the committee agreed: "There is cooperation on the committee on a lot of things, but on the major issues the Democrats will be found to protect their own party in the Post Office Department."

After minimizing the importance of partisanship, one representative added a distinction which gave his original answer some perspective:

Normally I would minimize the importance of partisan-
ship on this committee. Sure it makes a difference if the
Democrats control the presidency and the Congress. It's
not of great importance in the working of this commit-
tee because the committee usually deals with low-key
issues, low-level issues. Partisan divisions are more likely
to appear on some highly controversial issues. Our issues
are not highly controversial and don't lead to the kinds
of conflict that appear elsewhere.

Most members found partisanship more relevant in explaining behavior at the committee level than at the subcommittee level. Still, the type of issue must be kept in mind. Although Republicans and Democrats sit on different sides of the aisle in the House chamber itself, and although each party has its own set of leaders and its own cloakroom, and although the committee hearing room is marked by Democrats on one side of the table and Republicans on the other, when the subcommittees meet and work, partisanship tends to be submerged. Almost all committee members from both parties supported this proposition.

The minimizing of partisanship in the subcommittees can be laid to several factors. First is the private, no-publicity-to-be-gained context of discussion and work on the subcommittees. "In committee itself, as the members talk among themselves, partisanship usually doesn't make a darn bit of difference. Partisanship is most manifest at the public level where the minority will get an assistant secretary before the committee and just give him hell.''

Second, direct face-to-face relationships over time tended to blunt posturing. Third, many of the more ostentatiously partisan congressmen simply did not spend much time on subcommittee work. Fourth, subcommittee chairmen often tried to establish rapport with the ranking minority member. Since other minority members usually defer to the ranking member of the subcommittee, controversy can thus be lessened.

But the partisanship often works beneath the surface. The minority members are usually not consulted until the going gets rough. The following statement by a subcommittee chairman sets the tone: ''The topics selected for emphasis by the subcommittee are normally those that I am interested in. I listen to all viewpoints, but sometimes the minority must be ignored. I try to minimize the impact of partisanship. It's easier to catch flies with honey.'' Another Democrat made the same point: ''The majority is fully willing to accept minority criticism of the administration when they are right, but they are not right very often. They sometimes are carping and politically biased, but when their criticisms are legitimate, they are accepted.''

The minority party perspective was different. A ranking minority member on the full committee complained:

> *We get little attention because we are so small. If a Republican makes suggestions that the majority finds acceptable, the majority takes credit for them. Many minority members recognize the facts of political life and tire from attempts to buck the system.*

One of his colleagues added: ''This is a frustrating business for Republicans. Republicans can oppose but they can do very little themselves. They become frustrated, they lose initiative, they lose interest, and they put forth less effort.''

Another minority member reinforced this point: "I do not propose investigations and studies that I am interested in because they wouldn't go anywhere. They wouldn't be accepted by the majority. The door would be slammed in my face."

At least one subcommittee chairman minimized the importance of this line of analysis:

> I don't pay attention to the Republican suggestions that they can't get things done that they want done because they will often make broad general requests such as for a broad, sweeping investigation of the Post Office. It really doesn't mean anything. It's just done for publicity and that is all there is to it.

The lack of minority impact is partly explained by the make-up of the minority itself. One member of the White House staff saw the minority as frequently quiescent: "This is often because the ranking minority member is relatively passive and plays along in the system." A veteran observer of the committee noted that the senior Republican member did not necessarily lead all of the minority members. A junior Republican member asserted: "If we were more organized, we might have some slight impact."

An important official in the Post Office Department doubted that much more oversight would occur if the Republicans ran the committee. He traced this judgment to the attitudes of the ranking minority member. However, if the Republicans ran the committee, they would be subject to greater pressure from the Republican party leaders in the House. Because the minority was divided and because potentially active minority members were more concerned with other committees, the potential for oversight was diminished.

Each of the factors discussed thus far provides some explanation of why the committee did or did not attempt to oversee. But throughout the discussion doubts arise as to whether these opportunity factors are themselves decisive.

Most of them seem subject to modification if the members desire to do so. Thus attention is directed to a final opportunity factor, member priorities. The hypothesis here is that the oversight which is done is strongly related to the priority that members give to the committee and to its work. This subject requires a chapter of its own.

Chapter 3 The Post Office and Civil Service Committee: Member Priorities and Oversight

Knowing the priorities of committee members may be crucial to understanding their willingness to attempt to oversee, but establishing these priorities is a substantial task. The most obvious method of doing so was simply to ask members to state their priorities. This line of questioning yielded fruitful results from many congressmen. But where the members themselves had not set their priorities explicitly, where they were inactive and wanted to conceal it, or where they were reluctant to answer for a host of other reasons, the information derived was less useful. The responses of the members themselves needed to be supplemented.

A useful method of doing so was to ask staff members, lobbyists, as well as other congressmen to offer their perceptions of member priorities. The information provided by these sources usually matched that given by the member himself. Especially where it did not, more indicators needed to be found. Indirect indicators of priorities were derived from data about how members get on the committee, how long they stay, why they stay, and why they leave. This type of indirect data was especially useful for the Post Office and Civil Service Committee, where the turnover was substantial. Another index was derived from looking at the percentage of freshmen on a committee. Still other inferences emerged from noting the multiple committee and subcommittee assignments of each member and asking him how he coped with this variety of responsibilities.

Members seldom sought a position on the House Post Office and Civil Service Committee. They simply accepted an appointment. A Republican commented: "Gerry Ford asked me to serve on this committee. I am here only because he wants me to be here." Another stated: "I didn't really choose this committee. It was assigned to me." Most Democrats expressed similar sentiments: "I really didn't want to serve on this committee but I'm here. You might say I acquiesced to the decision." Another Democrat commented: "I was assigned to this committee. I will get off of it as fast as I can."

Although originally pushed onto the committee, a few members, but very few, came to like the assignment. "I didn't have high-priority assignments, but I am now pleased with them and do not necessarily want to get off."

Hardly any members actually have sought appointment to the committee. Many interviewees cited the same example as the only one that they could recall. The member in question explained his reasoning:

My predecessor was on this committee and liked it. I am from a marginal district, and it is useful to have government employees working for you in terms of reelection. Besides I have a labor background myself and am interested in the welfare of government employees.

Members do not, then, usually come to the committee with much interest in its work. They arrive with little knowledge about committee activities. Many leave as soon as they can; for example, only six members of the committee in 1960 were still there in 1965. Charles S. Bullock III reported that from 1947 to 1965 the Post Office and Civil Service Committee received sixty-nine Democratic appointees, only twenty-one of whom remained more than one term.[1]

The realities of the recruitment process and the priorities given to service on the committee explain why vacancies on it were so frequent. The largest single group of members consists of those who leave the committee. Their reasons for leaving fall into three categories: (1) they received an opportunity to join a committee with a subject matter more interesting to them; (2) they saw the committee as having low political salience for them; (3) they found the committee inactive and dull.

Since few members requested this committee and so many left it, a substantial percentage of its membership consisted of persons with very little seniority. In his study of House committee assignments from the 80th to the 86th Congress, Nicholas A. Masters provided data indicating the extent of freshmen appointments to particular committees. During this period, more freshmen (fifty-seven) were appointed to Post Office and Civil Service than to any other standing committee but Veterans' Affairs.[2]

The results of this continuing turnover were substantial. The presence of uninterested members and large numbers of freshmen who were learning about all aspects of the legislative process at once added up to a majority who lacked the experience and the expertise essential to coping with the problems of the Post Office. The large number of freshmen on the committee had additional consequences. Freshmen are sometimes in a politically precarious position. A fraction of the few who develop an interest in the committee may not be reelected; thus, more turnover occurs.

Once on the committee, most members had to face the choices common in the Congress: how to allocate their time among formal assignments and many informal tasks. Multiple assignments compounded the task. About 40 percent of the members of the House were assigned to more than one committee in the 89th Congress: 174 members were assigned to two committees; 256 were assigned to one committee. (Two persons, the Speaker and the Minority Leader, were assigned to no committees.) In contrast, over 90 percent of the 25 members of the Post Office and Civil Service Committee were assigned to two committees. The exceptions were Chairman Murray and Congressman Krebs. (See table 1.) The problem in priority-setting between formal committee obligations was perhaps more acute for members of this committee than for most members of the House.

In the interviews, members were asked what priority they gave to their several committee assignments. When the evidence is sifted, one conclusion leaps out. Of the twenty-three members of the committee with more than one committee assignment, fourteen, or more than 80 percent, asserted that the Post Office Committee was their second priority. Only four considered it their first priority.

Most members of the committee were not happy about their assignment in the first place. The probability that they would show strong interest in and exert much energy on committee work, oversight included, was low. The Congress is like any other human group: Congressmen who were willing to work would be asked to do more than they could handle. Where a member set his priorities was vital in predict-

TABLE 1: House Members with Single Committee Assignments

	1961	1963	1965
Whole House	66%	64%	60%
Government Operations Committee	10	19	3
Judiciary Committee	69	60	66
Post Office and Civil Service Committee	10	12	12

Source: Data from Louis C. Gawthrop, "Changing Membership Patterns in House Committees," American Political Science Review, *LX, no. 2 (June 1966), pp. 366–67.*

ing what part of his burdened schedule would be given to the Post Office Committee.

Why did most members accord the committee second priority? One reason was simply a lack of interest in the subject matter. "Nothing is going on of any particular importance on the Post Office and Civil Service Committee. I think it's important to be where the action is." A second category of explanation was the relationship of committee work to political survival.

> *My subcommittee on _____ is my life blood. This is the most necessary subcommittee that I have to work on for the welfare of my constituency. I am relatively vulnerable in my work on this committee, so when it comes to reelection I must devote primary attention to it. I see studies that need to be done on the Post Office Committee, but I don't have the time to do it.*

A staff member for another representative described the dilemma confronting his boss:

> *What he did in this case where he was faced with two complex problems on his two committees was to run from one to the other as the discussion ebbed back and forth. But he usually has to give more attention to the _____ committee because problems of _____ are vital to his district.*

Another member indicated his choice: "What goes on in the _____ committee is vital, and I have to give my primary attention to it."

Little oversight emerged when member priorities were low. How important, though, is the factor of multiple committee and subcommittee assignments in explaining committee oversight or the lack of it? How many members saw some difficulty in allocating their energies as a result of multiple committee and subcommittee assignments? Almost all members felt that the time problem was real, but opinion divided rather sharply as to whether multiple assignments seriously interfered with congressional attempts at oversight. Most members interviewed believed that a shortage of time was an annoyance that did not provide a basic explanation of why more oversight was not done. Other explanations were more common. A minority member asserted that partisanship bred casual efforts at oversight. "The basic problem is the lack of inclination to investigate one's own political party when it controls the administrative branch." Another Republican agreed: "The basic factor is simply the fact that the Democrats don't want to oversee their agencies too closely."

A second group of members who saw few problems in oversight as a result of multiple committee responsibilities were those whom other members viewed as the most manipulative, that is, most oriented toward bargaining. The concerns of this group of four or five members, resulting from their conception of the political process, allowed little room for abstract contemplation of what needed to be done. Each event was a bargaining situation to be exploited for personal and group advantage. These members were not unique in this attitude. The mixture of substance and process, subject interest and immediate personal gain that is the stuff of politics was just a little leaner in one direction for them.

Many of the most experienced congressional staff members, some of the most analytically inclined interviewees in the executive branch, and some of the most articulate members of the Congress seemed to agree that the choices made in the allocation of time are more decisive than an absolute lack of time. The comments below, ranging from the sympathetic to the dispassionate to the ridiculing, all reflect this position:

> *No member has much time to look out for problems, to create problems. Each member is busy already, but he can always do more if he wants to. The schedule is flexible, and if sensitive problems impinge on the member he can handle them. But the member does not start a sys-*

tematic search for problems. Conflicts do occur from multiple obligations on several committees and subcommittees, but these can be worked out.

I am not adequately informed on all the situations that I am supposed to participate in. No congressman can be with the multiplicity of assignments. I give first preference to those subcommittees that I regard as most important. I can handle these.

The committee spends too much time on pay bills. The largest single item for time consumption in the last six years has been in the pay bill. This is not a matter of necessity; it is a matter of choice. Congressmen could be relieved of this burden if they wanted to so they could do other things. But congressmen don't want this because congressmen gain a great deal of influence with the organized employee groups through their consideration of the pay bill each year, and they want to keep this influence because the employee groups provide money, workers, and publicity—all of these things of considerable value in promoting legislative careers.

They set their priorities in such a way that they simply don't have time to handle the big questions. But they could if they really wanted to. They deal with details and trivia.

A member of the committee frequently cited as an outstanding legislator presented a related argument:

The 1946 Legislative Reorganization Act has been violated, in spirit at least. The act aimed at creating a group of specialists on each committee, each of whom could pay careful attention to overseeing the appropriate executive departments. The fact of multiple committee and subcommittee assignments makes it very difficult if not impossible for the members to become specialists.

The members who did stay on the committee merit particular attention because the senior members of the committee are most likely to determine the course of its activity. Why did they stay on the committee? What relation did these reasons have to the oversight activities of the committee? One group of "stayers" was coopted by early ascent to positions of power. This rapid rise tends to be more characteristic of low-status committees. A second-term congressman might find himself in a subcommittee chairmanship with the perquisites that accompany that position. One highly respected member of the committee pondered this problem:

> *I stayed on this committee because I rapidly rose to the position of subcommittee chairman. I now have considerable power and influence in that role. If I had a chance to get on a top-notch committee such as Foreign Affairs or Ways and Means, I would find it very difficult to make the choice at the present time.*

These members frequently found it possible to gain a measure of influence on this committee while still giving a higher priority to another committee.

A second group of members remained on the committee to protect specific interests important to their constituency. The committee was likely to carry a second priority for them also. Representative Spark M. Matsunaga (D.–Hawaii) explained:

> *My first interest is agriculture because of the nature of my constituency. On the other hand, I am on the Post Office Committee for a very specific reason. There are thirty thousand federal workers in my state. Of these some fifteen thousand are affected by the 15 percent cost-of-living factor or addition which is provided. I got on this committee specifically to keep that, and I have been successful in doing so. I find it much easier to work from the inside than from the outside.*

A third group of members found the pace of the committee appealing. These members, who had primary concern for another committee or who had a strong desire to concentrate on noncommittee work in the Congress, found a comfortable home on the Post Office and Civil Service Committee. They rarely functioned as effective committee leaders. They tended to make a modest mark, both in the lawmaking and in the oversight aspects of the legislative process. One such member, when he died, received a ten-inch United Press International obituary which did not even mention his service on the Post Office Committee.

A fourth group stayed largely because the committee had high political salience for them in building support for campaigns and reelection. Since almost all congressmen act in a context of personal survival, it can be presumed that individuals or groups who contributed substantially to the reelection efforts of members would potentially have some impact on their subsequent behavior. Thus we come to the discussion of one of the most crucial factors in explaining committee behavior—in oversight and elsewhere—the relationships of members of the committee with interest groups, especially the government employee associations and the organized mailer groups. While these groups did not control the committee in any sinister fashion, the network of relationships between these interest groups and the committee helped to explain much of what the latter did or did not do.

The interest groups most relevant to the work of the Post Office Committee are old and established. A master list of such groups compiled by a committee member identified fifteen groups of postal employees alone. Also listed were twenty-five "other federal employee groups." A third category showed eleven "skilled trade and related groups." Under the heading "major organizations concerned with parcel post," thirteen groups appeared. In a final category, "major mail users concerned with zip codes," twenty groups were listed. The large number of groups may merely indicate that the United States is a society highly organized for political action. These numbers indicate, in addition, that organized interests have a substantial concern with the work of the Post Office and Civil Service Committee. This fact became unusually significant when contrasted with the level of public attention to the committee and with the priorities that the members themselves assigned to the committee.

Prominent among these groups was the National Association of Letter Carriers (NALC). Founded in 1889, the NALC in the mid-1960s had more than 175,000 members and approximately 6,400 local branches. Powerfully organized and intensely politically minded, the NALC has a long history of activity in the legislative process. Symbolic of this is the treatment accorded the first legislative champion of higher pay and better working conditions for mail carriers, Congressman Samuel Sullivan "Sunset" Cox, who served in the Congress between 1857 and 1889. Representative Cox is still heralded in NALC literature: "He is still reverently remembered by the NALC and his grave is decorated every year by members of Branch 41, Brooklyn, New York."[3]

Not only the carriers, but the postal clerks, the postal supervisors, the mail handlers, the star-route carriers, and the special delivery messengers, among others, have formed employee organizations. Basic to understanding the effectiveness of such groups is that some 90 percent of postal employees were organized in 1965, an unusually high percentage for government employees. Each of the major employee groups had a Washington, D.C., office; the few most active politically had a legislative representative who was better known on Capitol Hill to more members of the Congress and to more staff members than some assistant postmasters general.

If the cement of politics is support given and support withheld, then the ties of the employee groups to the members are strong and durable. Support was provided in the form of publicity, workers for campaigns, and money.

Much of the office staff time of many members of the

Congress is devoted to activities which directly or indirectly bring publicity and hopefully prestige to the congressman. A news conference which lasts fifteen minutes may take three days to prepare. A two-page newsletter to be mailed to constituents is the major item in the work week in some congressional offices. For many members of the Congress, the thirst for publicity is insatiable. Individuals or groups who can regularly provide favorable publicity at least have an entrée to the congressman. The postal employee groups are masters at promoting visibility for legislators, both formally and informally.

Formally, each major organization publishes a magazine for its members. Often printed on glossy paper and ornamented with photographs, these magazines feature pictures and stories about the work of the members of the Post Office Committees in the House and Senate. For example, three issues of the *Postal Record*, the monthly magazine of the NALC, carried the following: in March 1966, cover pictures of Post Office Committee members Morris K. Udall (D.–Arizona), Arnold Olsen (D.–Montana), and James Morrison; inside, pictures of committee members Glenn Cunningham (R.–Nebraska), Thaddeus J. Dulski (D.–New York), and also of Wilbur Mills (D.–Arkansas), Chairman of the House Ways and Means Committee. The issue also contained a list of relevant legislation introduced and the sponsors of these bills.

In April 1966, pictures of Representatives Udall, Dante B. Fascell (D.–Florida), Claude Pepper (D.–Florida), and J. J. Howard (D.–New Jersey) appeared. In May 1966, the cover featured a full-page picture of Senator A. Willis Robertson (D.–Virginia). Inside were pictures of Senators Robertson and Jennings Randolph (D.–West Virginia). Representatives Joseph Resnick (D.–New York), Cunningham, and John V. Tunney (D.–California) were also pictured, as were Representatives Morrison and Charles Wilson (D.–California). In addition, a picture was carried of some thirty congressmen who attended a legislative breakfast. In April 1966, a special issue of the *Record* dealt with a legislative service conference which some two thousand people attended. Page 89 featured a picture of congressmen referred to as "Congressional Champs."

The inside cover of the June 1966 issue of the *Postal Supervisor* listed birthday greetings to congressmen. Nine members of the House and Senate Post Office and Civil Service Committees were named. Equivalent publicity ran through related periodicals and newsletters. A partial sample of these publications, as of 1965–1967, is listed in table 2.

TABLE 2: Postal Employee Organizations' Periodicals

Organization	Magazine	Newsletter
National Association of Letter Carriers	Postal Record (monthly)	None
National Postal Union	Progressive (monthly newspaper)	Washington Report (weekly)
National Alliance of Postal and Federal Employees	National Alliance (monthly)	National Alliance Reporter
National Organization of Postal Supervisors	Postal Supervisor (monthly)	Newsletter (biweekly while Congress in session)

Yet another method of gaining recognition and publicity for favored members was to invite them to speak at association meetings, to give them awards for effective service, and to publicize these proceedings. For example, this item appeared in the *Pittsburgh Press* for April 30, 1967:

Dinner to Honor Rep. Corbett

Rep. Robert J. Corbett, Ben Avon Republican, will be honored by the Western Pennsylvania Postal Supervisors at their second annual dinner meeting Saturday at the Harbor House, Oakmont.

Bruce W. Sterling, vice president of the National Assn. of Postal Supervisors, will present an award to Mr. Corbett for his service as a member of the House Committee on Post Office and Civil Service.

Edward G. Coll, Pittsburgh postmaster, will be toastmaster. Martin Kundar Jr. of Beaver Falls is general chairman.

With the mechanization of society and the evolution of radio and television as major sources of news and gossip about politics, it is difficult to argue seriously that the mailmen through word of mouth are a major source of political information for many people. Yet even today, in some rural areas, mail carriers are a major link in carrying gossip and opinion to lonely housewives. This is one sense in which congressmen gain informally from their good works for postal employees.

Representative Morris Udall of Arizona is widely known in the Congress as a diligent and intelligent member. Yet if his constituents are at all typical, they probably know him better as a result of publicity frequently offered by postal employees and their organizations than as a result of his contributions to the legislative process. Of course, as chairman of the Compensation Subcommittee of the House Post Office and Civil Service Committee, Udall was no ordinary congressman from the point of view of the postal employees. As he expressed it:

> *It is a great help in my constituency to be on this committee. Everyone knows me partly because of the postal workers. Postal workers permeate the community. Not only that, but they organize their wives into ladies' auxiliaries that are not covered by the Hatch Act. When I go into a small town or rural area, people have heard of me*

*who haven't even heard of my brother [Stewart, then
secretary of the interior]. Here I am, one member of
Congress, and they know me because news of my work
is spread by the postal workers.*

In addition to publicity, the postal workers provide
assistance in reelection campaigns to congressmen who have
voted "right." The provisions of the Hatch Act are widely
interpreted to place an absolute wall between most government employees and the political process. This general impression is only partly accurate and largely irrelevant in
explaining the assistance which postal organizations provide
to legislators. Whether postal workers adhere religiously to
the provisions of the Hatch Act is a study in itself. But even
assuming that they do, a wide range of political activity is
still permitted them. Also, their wives are untouched by the
Hatch Act in their political involvement.

The restrictions on postal workers in political activity
still permit employees to attend political rallies and join
political clubs, to make voluntary contributions of money to
the party or candidate of their choice, to wear campaign
buttons and display bumper stickers, and to encourage others
to register to vote.

If federal employees are limited in their political activity, their wives are not. Recognizing this fact of life, the major
organizations of postal employees organized women's auxiliaries, in part to provide an effective legal vehicle for indirect
participation of government workers in partisan politics. In
the July 1966 issue of its magazine, the National Alliance of
Postal and Federal Employees ran a two-page set of questions
and answers about permissible political activity. Question and
Answer No. 12 are illustrative: "May a government employee's wife who is not a government employee engage in
political activity? Answer: Yes. The Act does not restrict the
activities of an employee's wife or other members of his

family in any way." Thus, a ready, reliable source of political support in campaigns is available to the candidate who has demonstrated his concern for the welfare of the postal workers. The following report in the *New York Times* suggested the value of such support:

> *Senator Ernest F. Hollings, South Carolina Democrat, took special pains to include the letter carriers on his Tuesday itinerary. Mr. Hollings was beaten by more than 100,000 votes in the Democratic primary in 1962 by the late Senator Olin D. Johnston, a staunch supporter of Postal Employees who received heavy state wide support from the mailmen and clerks.*[4]

Financial contributions from employee groups to congressmen are harder to document but are widely assumed to exist. Direct campaign grants to members are elusive; the generous participation of these groups, through purchasing tickets and contributing organizational skills, in testimonial dinners for favorite members of the Congress is widely acknowledged. The magazines and journals of the employee organizations frequently record that a testimonial dinner was held for a given member of the Congress. The participation of the group in this affair is then prominently noted. Perhaps as a way of building their own support with their members, employee group officials manage to be pictured with key congressmen across the pages of their house organs. It would be most difficult to determine the precise amounts raised at these affairs, but their continuing use indicates that a valuable service is seen as being performed.

Only rarely do these dinners, so frequently discussed in group publications, manage to hit the pages of the daily newspapers. One such incident widely reported across the country concerned the then newly selected chairman of the committee, Congressman Thaddeus J. Dulski. In 1965 in Buffalo, New York, a testimonial dinner was held, not to assist him in a campaign for reelection but, in the congressman's words, "as a personal tribute." Newspapers heralded the fact that Congressman Dulski had admitted that he had deposited some eleven thousand dollars in proceeds from this dinner.

The whole issue of testimonial dinners and congressional ethics is a fascinating one which has worried commentators as well as members of the Congress. One member of the Post Office Committee, widely known as the beneficiary of frequent testimonial dinners, anticipated questions by insisting that these dinners were perfectly honest because he used all of the proceeds for campaign purposes and not for himself. Whatever the merits of his contention, the immediate interest in the present context is not the broader question of congressional ethics, but the insight gained into the activities of employee groups and the utility of these activities for members of the Congress.

The Dulski dinner, his first one incidentally, was of less interest for itself than for the facts that emerged in subsequent writings about it. In an article in the *Wall Street Journal* for August 9, 1967, which broke the story, the following facts and judgments, commonly discussed previously among committee members and among those who observed them, became public knowledge. Postal employee groups were described as putting on "intense, sometimes savage pressure." Interest groups concerned with committee decision-making, in this case apparently mainly the direct mailers, had helped to locate ticket purchasers and to address invitations.

A direct correlation between these contributions and congressional decision-making cannot be drawn and in most cases probably should not be drawn. Representative Dulski stated the situation accurately: "Some of the same guys who bought tickets are nailing me to the cross for ingratitude." If direct correlation is clearly risky, it is equally obvious that interest groups involved in assisting members of the Congress felt that their efforts were worthwhile. The specific worth of their efforts will be discussed shortly. Observers of the committee asserted that testimonial dinners were quite common for key committee members, certainly for subcommittee chairmen.

Even more difficult to document than the number of testimonial dinners and the financial returns from them are the contributions that groups could make to the well-being of the members by providing transportation, theater tickets, and other forms of entertainment. Probably less discussed than testimonial dinners, these types of contributions helped demonstrate the good will of the groups involved.

The employee groups and the mailer associations did not make their efforts toward building good will without purpose. What did they want from the Post Office Committee? Perhaps the clearest and most succinct statement in print of what the employee groups asked from the Congress could be found in the *Branch Officers' Guide*, published by the National Association of Letter Carriers:

> *The NALC has been the acknowledged leader in winning 19 different pay raises for the postal and federal employees. There have been 17 retirement laws passed since that time [1920]—each because the NALC leadership [was working toward] . . . improving the economic lot of retired Government workers.*
>
> *There have been innumerable other pieces of beneficial legislation which the NALC has made possible. A few of the major laws in this category include:*
>
> *The Sunday closing law (1912); the 8-in-10 hour work law (1912); the Lloyd-LaFollette anti-gag law (1912); Workmen's Compensation Act (1916); the Compensatory Time laws (1916, 1920); shorter work week (1931); the Federal employees Life Insurance Act (1954); the Uniform Allowance (1954); the Federal Employees Health Benefits Act (1959); the Federal Pay Reform Act establishing the Principle of Comparability*

*in Government wages (1962); and the Provision for Sub-
stitute Overtime Pay (1965). In all, it is estimated that
approximately 110 pieces of major legislation benefit-
ting letter carriers and other postal and Federal employees have been signed into law during the twentieth
century to date. The NALC has been either totally or
primarily responsible for each of these bills. (pp. 4–5)*

Looking to the future, the *Guide* states:

*Of course, the NALC is not complacent or satisfied
now, and will never permit itself to be so. There are
many fields in which major advances are yet to be made.
We have not yet, for instance, been able to achieve true,
contemporary comparability for postal workers with the
salary structures for similar jobs in private industry.
There is still much to be done in the labor-management
field. There are improvements to be made in working
conditions. There are still inadequate attitudes toward
service in the top management which must be eradicated
and improved. There are still existing in the postal service some antiquated concepts of supervision. And so on
and on. (p. 6)*

This statement, with minor exceptions, characterized
the objectives and behavior of the major employee groups.
The primary focus was direct economic gain and improved
conditions of work. This conclusion, drawn from the formal
statements of the groups, was confirmed by interview responses from congressmen, lobbyists, and officials in the Post
Office Department. As one committee member put it:
"These groups respond to pay raises, and this is what they are
concerned with—benefits, working conditions, retirement,
and so forth."

One assistant postmaster general commented, "The employee groups probably get a great deal of what they want
because they've focused completely on a few things." A

lobbyist for an employee organization who has a reputation for being more concerned than most with broad questions of public policy asserted:

> *The resources of my union are tied up essentially in dealing with the salary question. We do not view other general problems of the operation at the Post Office as high-priority items. Our resources are limited and we tend to focus almost completely on questions of salary, retirement benefits, and related kinds of issues.*

Whatever their impact, these groups exerted efforts toward results in a narrow-gauged, clearly defined set of issues. Unlike such unions as the United Automobile Workers, the postal employee groups did not view their lobbying mission in the broad context of the welfare of society. A similar analysis holds for mailers' associations. Given this restricted focus, how did these groups move to achieve their objectives?

Their most prominent tactic was building political friendships among members of the Congress and particularly among members of the Post Office and Civil Service Committees in the House and Senate. The techniques of political support previously described are tendered in an implicit exchange for congressional support of group concerns.

The second tactic used was to build a skilled, well-financed lobbying organization to get the viewpoints of the groups across to congressmen. Table 3 shows that some employee groups devoted substantial sums to the lobbying effort. These figures should be read with caution because reporting requirements are vague and poorly defined. Two likely consequences are that the reported expenditures are seldom equal to the actual total expenditures for lobbying and that many groups with heavy expenditures for indirect lobbying do not feel bound by provisions of the law to report.

A third tactic was to testify before congressional committees on measures related to group interests. Post Office

TABLE 3: Expenditures Reported by Post Office Lobbyists

	1963	1964	1965	1966	1967
National Association of Letter Carriers	$62,202.17	$60,930.78	$66,487.39	$69,732.72	$133,877.00
United Federation of Postal Clerks	202,996.97	131,912.89	175,365.09	286,971.94	277,524.00
National Federation of Post Office and Motor Vehicle Employees	0	0	0	0	0
National Association of Postal Supervisors	30,822.22	28,924.09	46,733.28	34,153.20	39,344.00
National Association of Postmasters of U.S.	6,840.00	1,710.00	0	0	0
National Association of Post Office and Postal Transportation Service	0	0	0	0	0
National League of Postmasters	0	0	0	0	0
National Rural Letter Carrier's Association	36,099.59	59,364.21	51,123.77	43,369.98	25,611.00
National Star Route Mail Carrier's Assoc.	0	0	0	0	0
National Postal Union	57,300.00	0	0	0	0
National Association of Post Office and General Service Maintenance Employees	2,561.71	0	0	0	0

continued

TABLE 3—Continued

	1963	1964	1965	1966	1967
National Association of Special Delivery Messengers	0	0	0	0	0
National Alliance of Postal and Federal Employees	0	0	0	0	0
Post Office Regional Employees Association	0	0	0	0	0
Mutual Association of Postal Employees	0	0	0	0	0

Source: Data from the Congressional Quarterly Service, Legislators and Lobbyists, 2d ed. (Washington, 1968), pp. 32–40. This table was compiled by Louise Royster Brown.

Committee watchers are familiar with the rituals of committee hearings where the major groups were received with great interest and much deference as they provided data and analysis that were highly regarded by most members of the committee. Illustrating this procedure, the National Postal Union reported the following to its members in its magazine:

> *Slamming the short-comings of H.R. 14122, the pay-fringe bill passed by the House, NPU's resident officers on April 26 x-rayed its inadequacies and exposed previous testimony by administration spokesmen. Union officers delivered their dramatic criticism in the closing hours of the Senate Post Office Committee hearings, just before the Committee adjourned to go into executive session.*

A fourth tactic was to hold breakfasts for legislators where the representatives of the organizations could discuss affairs of state with many congressmen. The *Postal Record* for March 1966 reported: "Our state organizations hold salary breakfasts with Senators and members of the House of Representatives. At these rallies we tell the Congressmen how far the postal employee is behind private industry."

The New York State branch of the NALC noted in the April 1966 issue of the *Postal Record:* "Final arrangements have been made for our annual Congressional breakfast. . . . Invitations have been sent to all Congressmen and to both US Senators. Most of them are expected to attend." The Pittsburgh, Pennsylvania, chapter, after thanking the four Pittsburgh area members of the Congress for previous support, recorded, "We'll have an opportunity to meet with them when the Pennsylvania State Association holds its annual Congressional breakfast." The *Progressive* stated in February 1966, "NPU's legislative program was followed up at NPU's congressional get-together in the new Senate Office Building."

The *Postal Clerk* displayed over several pages many

pictures of friendly congressmen at the three-day National Legislative and Grievance Conference held in Washington in 1965. In a speech to the conference, Jerome Keating, president of the NALC, exhorted: "You are a shot in the arm of the Congress. You must stir them up, create their interest, create new interest. In this complex world with so much legislation before Congress, you have to make a noise to attract attention. This is why you are here."[6]

Beyond getting the postal employees' message before the congressmen, these conferences provided an opportunity for public praise of appropriate members of the Congress. Senator Ralph Yarborough (D.–Texas) was described as providing "unfailing support": "We have never had a better friend." Such conferences also enabled members of Congress to tell the assembled employees about the high quality of the Washington representatives of their organizations. With due allowance for the flourishes in rhetoric demanded on such occasions, the following comments by Representative Spark Matsunaga on the leadership of the UFPC illustrated the point: "Your representatives on the Hill certainly have no cause to fold up their tents—in fact, with the kind of leadership you now have, the UFPC may be entitled to a permanent edifice erected as a monument to their success in their working relationship with the Congress."[7] Or, in the words of Representative Morris Udall,

> *When members of the National Association of Letter Carriers pay their dues they are making the best investment they ever made in their lives. I don't know and don't care how much your dues are, they are still a bargain in comparison with what you get in return from your organization. Yours is the organization which delivers the most and you deliver it honorably and effectively.*[8]

A fifth tactic of the employee groups was to attempt to arouse their members to petition and otherwise pressure their congressmen. Most organizational leaders, noting the restricted power of Washington lobbyists as compared with an outpouring of sentiment from a member's constituency, regularly urge their members to make their views known in Washington. In addition, the groups through their publications alert their members to the needs for particular letters at specific times with regard to given legislation.

The NALC *Branch Officers' Guide,* reflecting the fruits of long experience, devoted three pages to letter writing. These pages, because they reflect the political astuteness of NALC efforts, are reproduced in part below:

Q. What are some useful tips for effective letter writing?

A. Keep the letter short and confine it to one issue. (A Congressman receives about 300 letters, on the average, per day. A senator may receive 2,000 letters a day. It helps to make your letter easy *to read.)*

Show, in the first paragraph, that you know what you're talking about by mentioning the Number of the Bill (if possible) and a brief description of its contents, such as "Postal Pay Reform," "Increasing Annuities for Federal Retirees," etc. Do not just say that you are in favor of a pay increase. Say that you are in favor of a specific Bill. *Keep the letter respectful and polite. Abuse and anger in a letter will merely irritate and perhaps antagonize a Congressman.*

Never threaten to vote against a Congressman if he votes against legislation. The support of Members is not "bought" in this way. An approach like this could very well make an undecided Congressman feel honor bound to vote against you. He already knows that you could conceivably withdraw your support from him if he votes against you. There's no need to remind him. (Some of the best friends of the N.A.L.C. in Congress used to vote against us. You catch flies with honey, not vinegar.)

Q. Can letters be "FAKED"?

A. Absolutely no. This would be fatal. If just one

phoney letter is detected, then doubt is cast on the authenticity of all the others. Signing someone else's name to a letter could also cause trouble with the Postal Inspection Service. During the 88th Congress, on a matter not related to the Post Office, a public relations operator picked a lot of names out of the telephone book and signed them to telegrams to a certain U.S. Senator. The ruse was immediately detected and exposed in the Congressional Record. The legislation was doomed, perhaps pemanently.

Q. When should a member write to Congress?

A. You should take your cue from the POSTAL RECORD, N.A.L.C. Bulletins and from your own national and local leaders. Usually, serious letter writing campaigns do not begin until after a particular Bill is introduced in one of the two Houses of Congress. However, there are no hard and set rules on this. But, of course, it would serve no useful purpose to write a Congressman urging his support of legislation that hasn't been introduced as yet.

REMEMBER:

DO write naturally, in your own language. Write as you would talk.

DO be friendly and persuasive, even if the Congressman has a record of being against our legislation.

DO be truthful in stating your case. Exaggerations hurt rather than help.

DO mention the correct Bill number and details of legislation.

DO keep your letters short and to the point.

DO keep your letters legible and easy to read.

DO sign your letters and add your home address so the Congressman will know you are his constituent.

DO be sure to get the spelling of your Congressman's name correct. Nothing irritates a politician more than getting his name wrong.

DO get all your family and all your friends to join you in writing letters when a campaign is in progress. Volume is important, even more than content. *(pp. 49–52)*

An example from the *NAPS News* of June 16, 1966, illustrated the second and more pinpointed approach: "We ask each member to write letters to their two Senators, immediately requesting their help in having HR 14122 voted upon immediately" (p. 1). Many congressmen acknowledge the substantial impact of letters resulting from these organizational appeals.

At times, group leaders even urge their members to lobby in person. The *New York Times*, on May 1, 1967, reported the fruit of such an appeal during the 1967 legislative struggle over a pay bill, noting that some thirty-five hundred mailmen had arrived in Washington and had spent "two days roaming Capitol Hill, seeing Congressmen and sitting in on the hearings."

In a more colorful, if probably less effective tactic, the National Postal Union, during the 1969 controversy over a proposed pay raise of 4 percent, expressed their contempt for the small increase offered by sending bags of peanuts to many congressmen labeled: "Nuts to 4.1%!"

If these tactics were the stuff of interest-group efforts, what effects did they have on the behavior of the House Post Office and Civil Service Committee? The most crucial impacts seemed to be in four areas: the agenda and time of the committee, committee information sources, committee staffing, and the committee decision-making process broadly conceived.

Committee Agenda and Time

The disarray of the postal service was no mystery to readers of national magazines or to users of the service itself. Yet the primary attention of the House Post Office Committee has seldom been systematically addressed to the problems of information and mail transmission in a highly complex industrial society. While the committee from time to time has delved into the fringes of central questions, it has not dealt directly and incisively with the fundamental problems of the postal service. What has occupied the time of the committee in recent years has largely been two items: the pay bills and the postal rates bills. Implicitly accepting the values of the interest groups ("the passage of a pay bill is always the most dramatic element in each legislative campaign"), the committee largely permitted the concerns of these groups to govern its allocations of time and energy. Two factors contribute to an explanation: first, the political leverage of the interest groups and second, the priority that the members give the committee's work. Since those members who chose to stay on the committee did so at least partly because of their relationship with the interest groups, group demands were given great attention. The interests of the employee groups were explicitly focused on material gains for their members; thus, one major thrust of the committee was in this direction.

Since the committee generally had low priority for those who ran it, with the exception of those who stayed largely because of interest-group relationships, a vacuum was created into which group pressures easily flowed. Most members devoted little time or energy to creative and innovative work on the committee. By contrast, the demands of the interest groups were heavy, blunt, and intensive. Thus, the committee was pushed into the area of economic benefits for governmental employees.

The other major item on the committee's yearly agenda in the years under study was postal rates. Since the costs of the Post Office Department were rising steadily, the pressures for rate increases were substantial. Most directly and substantially affected were the users of second-, third-, and fourth-class mail. The relevant interest groups were vocal and articulate in defense of whatever preferential rates the status quo afforded them. For reasons similar to those that applied to the employee groups, the Post Office Committee reacted attentively to the requests of the mailers.

Thus the battles were joined. On one side sat the administration, resisting the demands of the postal employees for reasons of economy and pressing for rate increases to meet the problems of increasing costs. On the other side were either the employee groups, pressing for economic gains, or the mailer groups, seeking to keep rates down. In the center of these conflicts sat the Post Office Committees in the House and Senate, made up largely of members who did not think that these committees were very important. Thus, the de facto agenda of the committees tended to be set by the interaction of the administration and organized interest groups. The committees were basically accommodators, compromisers, and responders rather than innovators.

Under such circumstances, the barriers to extensive and systematic oversight were massive. The behavior of many members of the committee was strongly structured by external pressures; only rarely was an important personal priority involved. The role of the interest groups in structuring the time of the committees was hard to overplay. This conclusion is reinforced when the sources of committee information about bureaucratic action are examined.

Committee Information Sources

Many members of the committee asserted that the employee groups served as a major source, probably the major source, of information about the Post Office Department. Since the concerns of the groups were narrow, the information they generated that reached the desks of congressmen reflected this restricted vision. But when the groups were asked to do staff work for congressmen, they eagerly complied, apparently with accuracy and skill. As one congressman saw it: "We get better facts from the interest groups than from the Post Office Department itself. The groups are a prime source for providing information and complaints that lead to investigations and other studies." Another member agreed: "The employee groups are a crucial source of information that leads to investigations." Still another noted: "The unions are a big help to me. They get wind of situations that need correcting, they get the word to me, and I look into it."

The prose was far from deathless, but the following statement in the *Postal Record* for March 1966 portrayed the essence of the situation. "As we are getting a run around from the Department, all grievances should be sent through our Congressmen and our Senators so they can see at first hand what the situation is." Grievances ranged from racial discrimination in promotions to the changing of work shifts. In discussing an attempt to change the working hours of charwomen at the Pittsburgh Post Office, a newspaper stated: "It was reportedly the sixth time in the past twenty years that the Post Office has tried to change the work schedules for various reasons, but the women have opposed the change *and* received support from Congressmen and Senators."[9]

Congressmen frequently looked outside the Post Office Department for information. They viewed the department as highly enmeshed in politics and hence selective in its responses. By contrast, many viewed the interest groups as more direct and honest in the information they provided. Many members argued that while it was possible to pry information from the Post Office Department, requests sometimes had to be pressed vigorously before information was disgorged. In contrast, the interest groups were ready and eager to ferret out what the congressmen desired. Thus congressmen, as they perceived the situation, had practical incentives for appealing to the interest groups for information.

Committee Staffing

A third impact of the pressure groups was on committee staffing. Most members of the House Post Office Committee did not consider a shortage of staff as an important explanation of why the committee did not undertake more oversight. This was partly because interest groups served functionally as staff for the committee by providing much information and analysis. The consequences were several. Again, what came to the committee this way was largely what the groups wanted to come. Secondly, the opportunity existed for members who wished to do so to use their staff positions mainly for patronage purposes without much regard for what a staff member might add to committee effectiveness. This pattern could be seen in staff appointments. The senior staff members of the committee were highly regarded for their technical competence; some of the staff people below this level did not add the weight that their numbers might indicate.

The interest-group impact on the committee's work was considerable. The information the committee received, the alternatives it heard, the time spent responding to group complaints, and a basically sympathetic attitude toward the groups all added up to the inescapable conclusion that in a complex and often indirect way, the interest groups really did shape much of what the committee did and *especially what the committee did not do.*

Committee Behavior Generally

This assessment of the impact of pressure groups on committee behavior rests on a strong foundation. It is based on extensive immersion in the work of the committee, the activities of the Post Office Department, and the relationships of the interest groups with each. Beyond this considered personal judgment, several types of evidence fortify this conclusion. First, the perceptions of participants vary normally only in the precise strength of impact assigned. Consensus existed among those interviewed that the impact of groups was large. The following language from several members of the committee is illustrative: "The employee groups are really more important than the administration ultimately in affecting how this committee works." A majority member shared the sentiment just expressed by a minority member: "They probably have too much of an impact on this committee." Another majority member saw the role of interest groups as strong but not decisive: "When employee groups and the administration get into battles, the administration usually wins, but that is not always the case." Another majority member added: "They are a very powerful force."

Two senior committee Democrats were quoted in an NALC publicity release:

I don't know of any leadership of any organization that is greater than the leadership that your organization has and has had, for the 22 years I have been in Congress. You have a strong and powerful, and a moving force in the nation's capital. All postal and federal employees should get on their knees every night and give thanks for the strength of the National Association of Letter Carriers.

Every intelligent member of Congress realizes that the president of the National Association of Letter Carriers knows more about postal legislation than any man alive. They seek his advice, they seek his help; and he is always eager and ready to supply both those essential commodities whenever he is asked.

A staff assistant to a senior majority member summarized:

These groups are more important than perhaps they ought to be. These groups are intimately involved in all levels of legislative decision making including bill mark-up. They start by making complaints about post office behavior to Committee members. They also present proposals for change. They testify at hearings. They participate in the bill mark-up. They constantly lobby on their particular points. They pressure members to change their positions even after the members have agreed to proposals for compromise.

Top officials in the Post Office Department who were frequently locked in combat with the interest groups attested to their great impact. "The House Post Office Committee can be considered to be the business agent of the unions."

The top staff of the Post Office Department can be tied up for months dealing with situations that are really of no great overall importance to the running of this department, but they have to be tied up because of protests to the congressional committees by the employee groups about something or other.

You cannot escape from the fact that the unions and their auxiliaries in their political work are basic to the lives of the congressmen on the committee. The government employee groups are the single most powerful lobby on Capitol Hill. They get a great deal of what they want because they focus so completely on a few things.

The employee groups are as powerful a lobby as ever existed in United States history.

A former postmaster general shared these attitudes:

The postal unions cannot strike but they have a unique power that other labor unions might well envy. They have power where it counts—with Congress, the Post Office's big boss. Having thousands of local units, including some in each Congressional district, the unions are free to communicate directly with their employers who are also the men their members help elect to Congress. This approach is undeniably effective.[10]

The primary lobbyists for the employee groups con-
curred in these assessments of their impact: "The impact of
the employee organizations on the committee is substantial.
This is not hard to explain. The Post Office employees are
more organized into labor unions than any other government
employees. We get more benefits for our employees than any
other groups in government. We get them first, the others get
them later. We often get results by presenting problems to
congressmen."

Newspaper writers who commented regularly on the
Washington bureaucracy and on its relationship with the
Congress agreed:

> *Outstanding—once again postal employee unions domi-
> nated the scene during the Senate Committee's delibera-
> tions on the Pay Bill. Several times the Senate group
> called in for consultation NALC President Jerome Keat-
> ing and Vice President James Rademacher.* [11]

> *The legislative achievements this year are something for
> which to be extremely grateful. Also, much credit
> should go to the various postal and federal employee
> union leaders and their organizations for the effective
> lobbying that helped achieve these results.*
> *Enactment of legislation simply does not "just
> happen." It represents tremendous lobbying skills and
> hard work on the part of employee union leaders.* [12]

> *NALC President Jerome J. Keating scored impressively
> in an appearance before the House Civil Service Com-
> mittee which is considering new salary increases for gov-
> ernment employees.* [13]

In his book, *The United States Postal Service*, Gerald
Cullinan concluded:

> *The influence of postal employees on Congress and the
> nation's press grew steadily during these years. Certainly
> the postal organizations were becoming more aggressive*

*in their attitudes. The newly elected president of the
National Association of Letter Carriers, William C. Doherty of Cincinnati, brought an original and modern
concept of trade-union leadership into the postal establishment. (Doherty dominated the postal labor scene
from his election in 1941 until his voluntary retirement
in 1962 to become the first U. S. Ambassador to Jamai-
ca. He and his capable successor, Jerome J. Keating of
Minneapolis, who served as vice-president of the NALC
for many years before his accession, have been called
the most effective lobbyists in the nation's capital.)*[14]

Comments and reactions to the report of the President's
Commission on Postal Organization, which advocated abol-
ishing the Post Office Department and substituting a government corporation, indicated also the perceived power of the
employee groups. For example, *Business Week* clearly viewed
the employee groups as potent political forces: "Overcoming
the opposition of the postal unions would indeed, be one of
the major obstacles facing the plan."[15] The consensus of
many reporters was reflected in these words: "But the major
obstacles to reform, without question, are the postal workers'
unions. They are among the most powerful lobbyists in the
Capitol and are likely to oppose Mr. Nixon's plan vigorously."[16]

Perhaps the most convincing corroboration comes from
the analysis of the House Post Office and Civil Service Committee developed by Richard F. Fenno, Jr., in *Congressmen
in Committees.*[17] Fenno used a scheme of analysis different
from the one here and came to an explanation of committee
behavior in passing legislation that parallels mine for committee oversight activity. He sees committee behavior in lawmaking as flowing from strategic premises shared by committee
members. These premises result from combining member
goals and environmental constraints. Fenno did not assess the
oversight behavior of the Post Office Committee.

The unanimity of competent observers in their judgments forms a reasonable basis for inference. Without an intimate and extended study of each pay bill and related matters, a totally authoritative judgment about pressure-group impact is not possible. But the purpose of this analysis is not to measure pressure-group impact with a slide rule, but to demonstrate that these groups have had a substantive impact on committee behavior.

Several additional bits of behavioral evidence reinforce the perceptual evidence which has formed the initial basis for judgment. One area relates to presidential vetoes. The norm of political behavior is that presidential vetoes are upheld by the Congress. The average percentage of vetoes overridden in all of United States history is less than 5 percent. In the eight years of the Eisenhower Administration, the president vetoed four postal pay bills; one of these vetoes was overridden by the Congress. Only two of Eisenhower's 169 vetoes were overridden altogether.[18]

Another indicator of group success was found in the use of the discharge petition, a method of moving a bill from committee for consideration by the full House. According to Gerald Cullinan, of thirty-one successful discharge petitions in American history, the NALC initiated six.[19]

From 1947 to 1953, "Congress passed sixteen laws favorable to postal workers. Three of the bills involved increases in pay; each was passed after a colorful legislative campaign and over administrative opposition."[20]

In many ways, perhaps the best single indicator of the impact of the employee groups was found in the statement of one committee member: "A distinction between pro- and antilabor is a basic determinant of attitudes on this committee as opposed to party affiliation or something of this sort."

Reviewing these opportunity factors provides an excellent foundation for an analysis of the oversight activities or lack of them of the House Post Office and Civil Service Committee. These factors indicate that a very low predisposition to oversee characterized the committee. Yet oversight activities were undertaken from time to time. One could anticipate most of these from the preceding discussion; a few others seemed almost idiosyncratic. But what mainly needs to be explained is why the committee conducted as little systematic oversight as it did. The major explanation was found in how members were assigned to the committee and in their priorities once they got there.

A Postscript

The passage of the Postal Reorganization Act of 1970 creating the U.S. Postal Service altered the context within which the House Post Office and Civil Service Committee operates. The Congress, and thus its committees, lost authority over the salaries of postal employees and over mail rates. Hence the basis for committee links with organized interest groups was eroded. The net effect was to remove a primary stimulus for committee action. Chairman Dulski, responding to charges that his committee didn't have very much to do, found it necessary in 1973 testimony before the House Select Committee on Committees to deny that the workload of his committee had decreased. Still, the gap between the formal workload of the committee and its actual behavior continued to pose a vexing problem.

Chapter 4 The Special Subcommittee on the Invasion of Privacy

The efforts at oversight by the Post Office and Civil Service Committee, discussed in chapters 2 and 3, were explained by factors largely institutionalized in the House: (1) a system of assignment to committees which placed freshmen on committees they did not seek; (2) substantial turnover in membership, since these freshmen were frequently eager to transfer from these committees as soon as they achieved a modicum of seniority; (3) the subsequent low priority that many members gave to the work of these unsought-after committees; (4) the links of many of those who remained on the committee to the powerful interest groups which hovered around it.

The House Government Operations Committee was more difficult to analyze as a unit because it was in essence a holding company for a series of subcommittees of uneven activity and effectiveness. The committee as a whole performed relatively few tasks. Much of the action was in the subcommittees. Therefore, to study one subcommittee does not wrench reality out of context. The relevance of the full committee lay primarily in the relationships between its chairman and the structure and behavior of the various subcommittees.

This chapter focuses on the oversight behavior of one subcommittee, the Special Subcommittee on the Invasion of Privacy (SSIP). The SSIP was born in 1964, with three members. It lived as a separate subcommittee through 1968. In 1969, it was absorbed into the Special Studies Subcommittee, chaired by Representative John S. Monagan (D.–Connecticut), as a "Special Enquiry." In March 1971, the SSIP and its successor disappeared from view. The SSIP, with its precarious existence from session to session, seemed an unlikely source of much oversight.

An assessment of the preconditions for oversight similar to that performed in chapters 2 and 3 would yield a low potential for oversight. Yet the SSIP produced substantial oversight. How is this seeming paradox to be explained? And what can be learned about legislative oversight from such an explanation? The seven opportunity factors presented initially in chapter 1 provide an organizing focus.

Legal Factors

All congressional committees have the obligation imposed by the 1946 Reorganization Act to oversee the executive branch. The House Government Operations Committee was given an especially firm legal mandate to oversee executive structure and conduct. Its jurisdiction in 1965–1967 was to: (1) handle "budget and accounting measures, other than appropriations"; (2) assess "reorganizations in the executive branch of the Government"; (3) receive and examine reports of the comptroller-general of the United States; (4) study "the operation of Government activities at all levels with a view to determining its economy and efficiency"; and (5) evaluate "the effects of laws enacted to reorganize the legislative and executive branches of the Government."

Generally, as noted previously, the legal authority to oversee did not translate automatically into oversight activity. An analysis of SSIP oversight efforts revealed little direct relationship between the Government Operations Committee mandate and SSIP activities. For the SSIP, the attitudes of the chairman of the full committee and of the SSIP chairman were better indicators of what the subcommittee's efforts might be.

The money provided for committee and subcommittee work can provide another indicator. More money available guarantees neither more nor effective oversight; adequate financial resources are a necessary precondition for some oversight. The financial resources of the Special Subcommittee on the Invasion of Privacy could only be described as meager. One would expect few results from a subcommittee which spent as little as revealed in Table 4.

An examination of legal powers, jurisdiction, and money available provided little indication that much oversight would come out of the Special Subcommittee on the Invasion of Privacy.

Staff Resources

Examining the second set of "opportunity factors," staff resources, only confirmed this trend. By no measure could the size of the staff of the SSIP be described as anything but modest. At times the formal staff consisted of only one person, who sometimes worked for another sub-

TABLE 4: Expenditures of the SSIP

Year	Expenditures
1964	$2,972.23
1965	25.25
1966	9.50
1967	2,794.30
1968	12,029.62

Source: Committee reports on expenditures filed pursuant to section 134(b) of the Legislative Reorganization Act of 1946 and published in the Congressional Record.

committee as well. At other intervals, the staff director, who frequently had only himself to supervise, had the part-time assistance of a secretary from the full committee staff. Office space was sometimes a desk in the crowded rooms of the full committee's facilities.

Tenure of SSIP staff members was short; rapid rotation in office was the norm. In four years, three persons with various titles held the position of staff director. This picture of staff size is slightly misleading for two reasons. First, the chairman of the SSIP used personnel from his own office staff to bolster the manpower supply of the subcommittee. For example, in the data bank study, Mr. Steven Eagle from the office staff of Congressman Cornelius Gallagher (D.–New Jersey) assisted in the preparation of the SSIP report.[1] Second, since subcommittees in the Senate had published the results of related studies, the staff of the SSIP could use these documents for leads and information.

Staff attitudes toward oversight are frequently a function of the attitudes of the members who appointed them. Several of the SSIP staff members were moved over from Congressman Gallagher's office staff. They reflected his energy and concern with invasion of privacy and, in some cases, even prodded the chairman into greater activity concerning invasion of privacy.

The impact of individual staff members was felt in three particular areas. The first was pressure for additional staff. Whatever his interest in the subcommittee, the chairman was beset by the multiple obligations that press all members of the Congress. If the mission of the subcommittee is large and if the staff is highly interested in pursuing questions vigorously, the member may find himself pressured by his staff to provide additional help. This was the case for the SSIP.

Second, where the mission of the subcommittee is vague, and it was for the SSIP, and where the chairman is not pushed to act by strong external pressures, as he was not on this subcommittee, then the topics selected for study may in essence be determined by the staff. The scope of invasion of privacy is massive; the staff often selected topics they regarded as crucial and "convinced" the chairman that these particular topics should be pursued. One staff member reported: "We received letters of complaint from citizens. Staff members then looked into it. I then wrote a three- to four-page memorandum to the chairman and convinced him that this was appropriate for a full-scale investigation."

Once a topic was selected for subcommittee investigation, the staff performed a third crucial function: selecting and screening witnesses and briefing committee members as to what to expect from the witnesses.

In this subcommittee, the small number of staff members would seem to indicate few opportunities for oversight, but this was offset in part by staff diligence. Although none of the three SSIP members regarded a shortage of staff as a basic explanatory factor, each acknowledged that there had been times when more staff would have been useful. Some consequences of the limited staff were seen in the inability to follow through on the problems uncovered and in the selection of topics to be studied. Congressman Benjamin Rosenthal (D.–New York) suggested in assessing the committee work on personality testing in the federal government: "When we presented our findings to agency heads, some changed their practices with very little resistance. The committee has typically not pushed where we have encountered much resistance. We don't have the time to always follow through."

Subject Matter

The subject matter with which the SSIP dealt was not sufficiently complex to impede rapid progress. Lie-detector examinations are seen by some as an arcane art, but one needs no massive technical knowledge to know that when applicants for clerk-typist positions are required to discuss intimate details of their sex lives, congressional attention may be warranted.

Disputes over invasion of privacy were often not technical disputes over esoteric scientific matters; they were more frequently concerned with either obvious misapplications of reasonable procedures or the conflicts of values which were resolved differently according to the priorities of various decision makers.

The first situation was illustrated in the governmental use of lie-detector tests for hiring employees. There may well be unresolvable conflicts over the scientific status of such tests and over where precisely it is appropriate to use them. These conflicts were not at the center of invasion-of-privacy investigations. Where some tests were administered in a manner seemingly designed to satisfy the voyeurism of the tester, then all that was required was that these practices be documented and exposed. Investigative energy and skill were more crucial than great technical competence.

In other situations, such as that involving the proposal for a national data bank, shared values were weighted differently by participants in decision-making. All participants regarded the protection of personal privacy, the need for effective research, and efficiency and economy in record-keeping as important. The root of the conflict was that the SSIP gave protection of privacy a higher priority than did the Bureau of the Budget.

> MR. GALLAGHER: *What we are looking for is a sense of balance. We do not want to deprive ourselves of the rewards of science; we simply want to make sure that human dignity and civil liberties remain intact. . . . The issue is, therefore, can we achieve a balance as to assure that technical progress will serve man and that man's free will will dominate in the new environment that the computer is rapidly bringing about.* [2]

MR. BOWMAN [Raymond Bowman, Bureau of the Budget] : While we want to do all that we can to bring all available statistical information to bear on any problem under study and while we are continually concerned with the need to reduce duplication by making the fullest possible use of existing statistical materials, we are also vitally concerned with preserving the confidentiality of the information reported to the Government.[3]

The hurdles posed by complexity of subject matter were neatly sidestepped in the SSIP hearings, as will be illustrated shortly.

The SSIP activities seem not to support the hypothesis that the likelihood of oversight is enhanced if the committee is concerned with an activity centered in a few departments, as opposed to policy-making diffused through the executive branch. Clearly, questions of invasion of privacy may arise in many different departments and agencies. Thus, the potential for effective oversight would seem to be lessened. The hypothesis about centralization of activity and effective oversight rests implicitly on the assumption of a large, coherent subject matter intricately intertwined into executive operations. Invasion of privacy does not fit this category. The subject may be examined by congressional committees quite apart from the overall substantive program of any single department or agency.

On many questions of invasion of privacy, the visibility of the issue involved was sufficiently high to relevant clienteles to enhance the opportunity for oversight. All three members of the SSIP acknowledged that they received much publicity, many requests to address groups, and other political bonuses from their work on the subcommittee. Especially helpful in explaining this visibility was the highly symbolic content of such issues as probing into sexual behavior, besmirching one's credit record, and prying into religious beliefs. Here was a series of visible, emotionally charged issues that provided psychic payoffs, if not concrete ones, from much of the attentive public.

In sum, the nature of the subject matter seemed to promote the possibility of legislative oversight. The broadness of the subject, however, would make a comprehensive effort unlikely.

Committee Structure

The structure of the House Government Operations Committee in 1965–1966 was conducive to oversight for subcommittees that wished to conduct it. Within loose but generally well-understood limits, subcommittees were free to pursue their own programs. This was a decentralized committee where the chairman of the full committee, William Dawson (D.–Illinois), ran a holding company for a series of seemingly disparate committee enterprises. Congressman Dawson did exercise enough potential power to command deference and attention from the subcommittee chairman. His name appeared in nearly all of the SSIP news releases. A second form of deference was exhibited in the regular SSIP habit of praising Chairman Dawson in print at every opportunity. For example, early in the hearings entitled *Special Inquiry on Invasion of Privacy*, Congressman Rosenthal noted:

> *I think the record ought to indicate that all of us are very grateful to Chairman Dawson for establishing this inquiry. His interest in the subject of privacy and constitutional rights of all of our citizens has been known by all the members of Congress for a long time. Certainly he has been a leader in the fight for the preservation of the individual rights under our constitution.*[4]

Similar statements ran through other committee documents and in Congressman Gallagher's frequent summaries of SSIP activity on the floor of the House.[5]

Attention to Chairman Dawson was in large part a recognition of his significant formal authority. This authority could be measured in the printed rules of the House Government Operations Committee for the 89th Congress. For example, Rule Three provided:

> *The chairman shall have authority to establish subcommittees and to assign to them such functions as he may deem advisable. The chairman shall have the authority to refer bills, resolutions, and other matters to appropriate subcommittees for consideration or investigation, and to recall such bills, resolutions, and other matters from the subcommittees to which they have been referred.*

Rule Twelve stated that "the staff of the committee shall be subject to the direction of the chairman and shall perform such duties as he may assign." Rule Fourteen asserted: "The chairman shall have the authority to hire and discharge employees of the professional and clerical staff of the full committee and subcommittees subject to the appropriate approval."

Committee decentralization meant, in this case, subcommittees with sharply differing behavior. Such highly prestigious and well-established subcommittees as that on military operations coordinated with the chairman of the full committee but in essence went their own way, with physical facilities separate from those of the full committee, with their own substantial budgets, and with separate staffs. On the other hand, the SSIP had to fight for its very existence and for its budget at the beginning of each session of the Congress.

The precarious status of the SSIP goes back to its origins in 1964. The SSIP was created under somewhat obscure circumstances. Involved were the desires of Congressman Gallagher to establish a subcommittee; an internecine dispute involving Gallagher; and Gallagher's participation in the work of the Subcommittee on Foreign Operations and Government Information as it studied the use of polygraphs. In Congressman Gallagher's words, "We need another outlet other than casework and letters for complaints."

Originally intended to be short-lived, perhaps to last until the end of 1965, its first full year, the SSIP somehow managed to be reconstituted during the 89th and the 90th Congresses in 1966, 1967, and 1968.

Reconstitution did not come easily. Congressman Gallagher was forced to spend considerable time lobbying with Chairman Dawson and with others for this result. "I have to spend as much time in the politics of keeping it going as in doing the work." Time and energy for oversight were decreased accordingly. Decentralization normally facilitates the ability of an eager subcommittee chairman to conduct oversight. In the particular circumstances of the SSIP, with its yearly fight for survival, this promoting factor was offset considerably.

Status on a Committee

A fifth opportunity factor relates to the members' status on a particular committee. For the SSIP, the fact that a highly interested member of the full committee had asked for the subcommittee to be created and that he then served as chairman certainly enhanced the potential for oversight. The three members of the subcommittee were not powerful decision makers on the full committee, nor was their seniority particularly high. In the 89th Congress (1965–1966), for example, on a committee of twenty-three Democrats and eleven Republicans, Representative Gallagher ranked sixteenth in seniority on the Democratic side and Representative Rosenthal ranked eighteenth. On the Republican side, Representative Horton ranked fourth. That the prime mover and chief figure in the subcommittee's work, Congressman Gallagher, was a recognized supporter of the administration and of Chairman Dawson did not hurt the cause of the subcommittee. Neither Gallagher nor Rosenthal, as befitted their low seniority, was the chairman of any other subcommittee on the Government Operations Committee or a chairman on any other standing committee or subcommittee.

Relations with the Executive Branch

The sixth set of opportunity factors, relations with the executive branch, was not crucial in explaining the oversight efforts of this committee. As a new subcommittee, this group had no established record of treatment by executive departments. Partisanship was not relevant, since the two Democrats and one Republican on the subcommittee agreed on the policies they wished to pursue.

The factor most relevant here was committee relations with top personnel in the executive branch. In most situations, and on most issues, rapport was quite good. The subcommittee operated on the assumption that top officials in the various departments were unaware that violations of privacy existed in their departments and agencies and hence would be willing to correct abuses if informed of them. That is, the members assumed that they could usually attain their goals by making top department officials and agency heads cognizant of problems that existed in their own areas. This assumption frequently turned out to be correct. As one official in the Department of Labor stated: "High officials in this department were not aware of the details of the personality testing being done. We now pass on the propriety of all testing. We didn't do that before."

Member Priorities

The final opportunity factor is member priorities. How important was the work of the SSIP to the members? How did each member rank his subcommittee and his committee?

What priority did he give to each specific issue that the subcommittee faced? For the SSIP, a rather mixed picture emerged. All three members of the subcommittee were more than nominally interested in its work. All were there because of this interest. No one was coopted into membership against his own desires. While none of the three members linked the work of the SSIP directly with his reelection chances, each did see political benefit from his participation: "I see no tangible evidence that my work on the subcommittee helps me in my constituency. I do get some personal publicity from it. My constituents probably do get the impression that I am active." "I get no direct, substantial benefit from my constituency for serving on this committee. I do get a few speaking engagements from groups that I would not have gotten otherwise. That may be of some benefit in my constituency. I get a little publicity from it. I issue news releases on the subject." "I get no substantial political gain from my work on the committee. My publicity releases do get some attention. It takes time, in fact, from wakes and picnics, both highly profitable political activities. But there are surely no political minuses in this committee work."

If each of the three representatives did not ignore the work of the SSIP, neither did he see it as his top priority among the various committees on which he served. Although the SSIP was Representative Gallagher's congressional child, his primary committee labors went to the Foreign Affairs Committee. The problems created by these dual loyalties were illustrated in a statement by Representative Gallagher during the SSIP hearings entitled *Retail Credit Co. of Atlanta, Georgia:* "I regret the delay we have had in these hearings and we appreciate your patience. The previous dates we had scheduled had to be cancelled because of hearings going on within the Foreign Affairs Committee."[6]

Representatives Rosenthal and Frank Horton (R.–New York) also had primary interests elsewhere. But each of the three members was so unusually energetic and hard-working that a second priority for them did not mean ignoring the SSIP. Rather it was another limit on what they could do. As one member noted, "The basic problem in explaining the lack of additional efforts is simply a lack of time of the members. Meetings of committees conflict. Conflicting obligations accrue in terms of working on legislation. Members simply cannot devote the time to oversight that they might want to in the abstract."

The extent of these formal obligations was indicated by the committee and subcommittee assignments of the three members. Congressman Gallagher was assigned to Foreign Affairs (three subcommittees) and Government Operations (three subcommittees). Congressman Horton belonged to the District of Columbia Committee (three subcommittees), Government Operations (three subcommittees), and Small Business (two subcommittees). Congressman Rosenthal was a member of Foreign Affairs (three subcommittees) and Government Operations (three subcommittees).

The record of extensive activity of the SSIP showed that the "congressmen are busy" hypothesis was an accurate but not a sufficient explanation of why congressmen did not oversee more aggressively. Parkinson's aphorism that work expands to fill the time available directs explanations of the lack of oversight activity to the question of how members allocate their time and energy.

All three members attended SSIP meetings faithfully, but what the committee did was what the chairman wanted it to do, and what he wanted it to do was influenced somewhat by the pressures the staff placed on him.

An examination of opportunity factors in chapters 2 and 3 predicted what the normal pattern of committee oversight activity would be. An equivalent pattern for the SSIP was more difficult to prescribe. Seemingly the SSIP had some factors which pushed oversight and some that seemed to retard it. Central in accounting for its activity were the interests of the chairman and of the staff.

Effectiveness in oversight by the SSIP was even more difficult to measure. In looking at the Post Office Committee, one could use as a yardstick recognition of fundamental problems in the Post Office Department and the attempt to study them and to influence change. For the SSIP, the boundaries of the mandate were so vague that one could not know precisely whether it had done its job. It is clear, however, that the SSIP has achieved concrete results in several important areas.

In the presence of a high propensity to oversee and yet given certain clear handicaps to systematic, intensive oversight, how did the factors work out in the types of situations hypothesized in chapter 1 as being relevant for the conversion of propensity into behavior?

Of the conversion factors discussed in chapter 1—disagreement or agreement on new policies, executive requests for major changes in existing programs, and the impact of sudden and particular events—the latter two seem most relevant in a discussion of the work of the SSIP. The SSIP concern with the proposal by the Bureau of the Budget for the creation of a data bank illustrated how a shift in policy promoted oversight. The issue of personality testing in the hiring of government employees illustrated the impact of specific events.

The Proposal for a National Data Bank

The predisposition of a committee or a subcommittee to oversee does not predetermine whether it will actually do so. The conversion factors discussed in chapter 1 help fill the gap between predisposition and behavior. The experience with the proposal for a national data bank illustrated these linkages.

The proposal for a national data center emerged initially as simply another routine device for promoting efficiency and economy. Instead, a volatile issue developed. In the early

1960s, the Social Science Research Council, in response to a request from the Executive Committee of the American Economic Association, formed a committee to consult with governmental agencies about the problem of making the mass of statistics gathered by government more readily available to serious scholars. Individual departments or bureaus within the government were simply not equipped either with funds or with personnel to meet the legitimate needs of the scholarly community. After some four years of preliminary probing, the Committee on the Preservation and Use of Economic Data (popularly referred to as the Ruggles Committee after Charles Ruggles, the Yale economist who chaired the group) reported in 1965. The Ruggles Committee recommended that a federal data center be created to facilitate the use of governmentally gathered data by both governmental and non-governmental users.

> *Because of the decentralized nature of the Federal statistical system and the pressure of the primary functions of the agencies, neither outside scholars nor Federal agencies are able to utilize efficiently the large amount of information which has been obtained at public expense.*
>
> *For the reasons ... outlined above, the Committee on the Preservation and Use of Economic Data urges that a Federal Data Center be established by the Federal Government to preserve and make available to both Federal agencies and nongovernment users basic statistical data originating in all Federal agencies.* [7]

The Bureau of the Budget, the agency responsible at that time for improving, developing, and coordinating federal statistical services, then asked Edgar S. Dunn, a former deputy assistant secretary in the Commerce Department, to study the entire question and to prepare a report on it. The Dunn Report, in November 1965, recognized the problems cited in the Ruggles Report and called for the establishment of a national data service center. What seemed to be happening was that a rather minor administrative change was in process, a change like thousands of others that are implemented routinely in the name of efficiency and economy.

The major focus of these two reports was technical. In each one, the discussion centered around questions such as feasibility and utility. The entire project seemed so routine that a close student of problems of information storage and retrieval could say: "At this writing [1965], the Budget Bureau *ad hoc* committee responsible for acting on the recommendations of the Ruggles Committee hopes to have funding for a Federal Data Center included in the budget for the fiscal year 1967."[8] A similar sentiment was reflected in the work of the task force set up by the Bureau of the Budget to study the problem. Formally titled "Task Force on the Storage of and Access to Government Statistics," the committee established in 1965 reported in October 1966. Writing in the Spring 1967 issue of *Public Interest*, Carl Kaysen, the committee chairman, noted: "They [the committee] certainly did not expect it [their work] to be controversial."[9] Even a sharp critic of the data bank proposal, sociologist Orville Brim, said in a speech in April 1966 that the data bank might only be two years away.[10] Nowhere in all of the reports was the issue of invasion of privacy discussed at any length or to any depth.

From the perspective of the Bureau of the Budget and others, the proposal for a national data center was merely another step along familiar paths. From the perspective of the members and staff of the SSIP, the proposal for a new data center presented a frightening development. Differences in executive and legislative perceptions of the problem proved to be a major basis for discord. The following colloquy illustrated the problem:

CONGRESSMAN HORTON: You are talking about a present system that is quite different from the system that you are now proposing or that you are at least considering.

MR. BOWMAN: I think that we are not proposing a system that is significantly different from the system we now have. We are proposing . . .

MR. HORTON: You may not feel it is that way but it seems to me that it is.[11]

In terms of a traditional definition of oversight, there was none here to be had. No existing structure, program, or personnel policy was to be examined to see how previous legislation was working. From a more functional perspective, there was plenty of oversight to be accomplished if the aim of the Congress or of its subunits was to influence bureaucratic activity. That, of course, was precisely the intent here. The point of the three-day hearings on the national data center held by the SSIP in July 1966 was not to check up on an existing operation, but rather through publicity and legal threat to gain considerable influence over the conditions under which an emerging structure would develop. As Congressman Gallagher noted in his introductory statement:

> *The subcommittee believes it is important that we consider this question before the establishment of a national data center or bank becomes a fact. What we seek at this point is to create a climate of concern, in the hope that guidelines can be set which will protect the confidentiality of reports and prevent invasion of individual privacy, while at the same time allowing government to function more efficiently and facilitating the necessary research of scholars in statistical analysis.*[12]

Mr. Bowman indicated a different perspective: "You see, this hearing is in a sense preliminary to any proposal that we are bringing before the Congress. We have not finished our job yet. We have not completed our review."[13]

As the SSIP hearings began, the shape of executive-legislative conflict became apparent quickly. Chairman Gallagher spoke of the development of technology and of the potential dangers arising from the computerization of modern life. He spoke of statistical materials being used or misused to form a dossier bank in which the privacy of individuals who had provided the government with information would be invaded as these data were stored in a central computerized facility. Vance Packard, the first witness, then testified about the threats to invasion of privacy which would come from the centralization of records.

Spokesmen for the Bureau of the Budget seemed initially unable to fathom the depths of concern with privacy by the SSIP especially, they argued, since no proposal or plan for a dossier bank on individuals was under consideration. Citing the success of other governmental agencies, especially the Census Bureau, in maintaining privacy and not revealing information gathered over the years, and emphasizing the fact that the proposed national data center was to facilitate statistical analysis and not to gather information and files about individuals, executive branch spokesmen asserted their concern with privacy. They expected to manifest this concern as they had previously, through the application of orthodox procedures developed and tested over time.

From the perspective of the SSIP, these traditional safeguards were simply not adequate. The SSIP made no detailed inquiry into the nature of these protections, but instead the members asserted and reasserted substantially the same four points: (1) Whatever the intended uses of the materials in the proposed data center, as long as individual identification remained on the records stored on the computer tapes, then the dangers to individual privacy were real. (2) Although such records were already kept, they were dispersed in some twenty departments. Decentralization and the inefficiency inherent therein were viewed as effective defenses against the invasion of privacy. Centralization, it was asserted, increased the danger of leaks of information. (3) The good intentions of the planners of the center were simply not sufficient guarantees against the possibility of invasion of privacy. (4) Insufficient manifest concern about privacy had been evidenced in the Ruggles and Dunn reports and in the presentations by the Bureau of Budget. None of the documents prepared by the Bureau of the Budget, the SSIP members asserted, took sufficient account of the problem. In the words of Congressman Rosenthal:

> *It seems to me that you fellows don't come in with clean hands if you hadn't considered that before you went to the trouble of printing all these documents and making this presentation. It would seem to me that that would be one of the first things I would have thought before I went so far along as you people have. What you are doing now is reacting to the interest of a congressional committee. I have some doubts as to whether you would have done this had this inquiry not been held. It would seem to me that your reputation would have been enhanced had you done this in the first instance on your own, of your own volition, and included it all in these documents and books that you have prepared.*[14]

In response, Mr. Dunn asserted: "I agree. . . . I was operating within a frame of orientation which said we were talking about the way in which we improve a set of established statistical services, and we are essentially operating within a tradition where we just take for granted that we have got to protect the personal."[15]

Whatever the original intent of the SSIP members in scheduling the hearings, the members of the subcommittee came to disclaim any Luddite intentions. The SSIP did not intend to take axes to the computers. They argued that no attempt was being made to bar the path of progress. What was being done was to make sure that the price of technological progress would not be too high as measured by the loss of privacy. Congressman Gallagher had stated initially that the purpose of the hearings was twofold: to publicize what was being planned so as to create a climate of concern about privacy, and secondly, to influence government guidelines that would be created for the operation of this center.

If scores of editorials and magazine articles and hundreds of letters were an index, then the attempt of the SSIP to stimulate concern about possible abuses arising from use of the computer was highly successful. In addition, several books dealt in some length with the issues raised in SSIP hearings.[16]

A national data bank was not yet in being in the early 1970s. The ultimate success of the SSIP in protecting the right to privacy cannot be firmly established. Yet developments did occur which in all probability would not have taken place in the absence of congressional involvement.[17]

The Bureau of the Budget agreed not to establish a center before an actual proposal was submitted to the Congress for its advice and consent. Before the congressional hearings had been held, it seemed clear that the Bureau of the Budget had planned simply to move ahead incrementally toward establishing a center.

> *MR. BOWMAN: At the present time we are merely considering this. It probably would be possible for an agency to take on some of the functions of the Data Center, but we have no intention of doing this without a proposal that would be officially presented to the Congress.*

> *MR. GALLAGHER: And we now have your assurance as part of a legislative record which we are trying to establish here, that when and if your studies are concluded, before you will go ahead, you will come to the Congress and request permission, is that correct?*

> *MR. BOWMAN: That is right.*[18]

The planners in the Bureau of the Budget were made painfully aware that a strong concern about the invasion of privacy existed among vocal and articulate members of the Congress. As a matter of political reality, a similar concern needed to be manifested in executive planning for the center. An early recognition of this need to be more explicitly concerned with the issue of privacy was seen in the so-called Kaysen Report, "Report of the Task Force on the Storage of and Access to Government Statistics," issued shortly after the SSIP hearings. In an annex, the Kaysen Report attempted to take into account the criticism made by the SSIP concerning the invasion of privacy.

New energy was stimulated in searching for means whereby the dangers to privacy from new applications of computer technology could be limited. Thus, on the issue of the proposed data center, the efforts of the SSIP were highly successful for several years in influencing policies of a segment of the bureaucracy.

An attempt to explain this apparent success sheds light on the problems of the Congress as it seeks to oversee the bureaucracy. The committee's readiness to proceed in this area needs to be explained. Why the executive branch seemed so prepared to respond in the face of pressures from so few members of the Congress and from members not high among congressional power holders also requires attention.

A review of the opportunity factors suggests several reasons why effective oversight should have been most difficult on the data bank issue. The first of these is the immense complexity of the subject matter. Three busy congressmen and a small staff meagerly endowed with funds seemed an unlikely source for sufficient expertise to tackle this massive issue.

But what should have been a major obstacle to effective oversight, the complexity of the subject matter, turned out not to be relevant at all to the SSIP efforts. The explanations are several. First, the SSIP did not define its mission as the study of information storage and retrieval procedures within the federal government. Thus, no expertise appropriate to that endeavor was required. The SSIP instead focused exclusively on the privacy aspects of the data bank. Because the data bank was perceived as a new, unprecedented situation, the committee treated previous experience in protecting privacy as irrelevant. Secondly, on the privacy issue, the members and staff of the SSIP were not congressional amateurs confronting the subject-matter experts in the executive branch. For all practical purposes, the more arcane aspects of how to build protections for privacy into information retrieval processes were subjects beyond any existing expertise. The following dialogue between Chairman Gallagher and Paul Baran, a computer expert with the Rand Corporation, illustrated this point:

MR. BARAN: It [invasion of privacy through the use of computers] is a very poorly studied problem. I speak to you with great ignorance today.

MR. GALLAGHER: If you speak with ignorance think of the position we are in.

MR. BARAN: That is right. We are all in the same boat.

MR. GALLAGHER: Do you think that the people who are suggesting this proposal are beyond this point of ignorance that the rest of us share?

MR. BARAN: I think we are all pulling on oars in the same boat.

MR. GALLAGHER: Do you think that they have a broader understanding of computer capacity than you and your fellow experts have?

MR. BARAN: I have not read their report, but from the remarks of yesterday they had not emphasized their

*examination of this problem. There is practically noth-
ing to be found in the computer literature on the subject.*[19]

Third, the SSIP focused heavily on the symbolic aspects
of the computer's impact on privacy. In the words of Congressman Rosenthal:

*My own personal reaction to the proposal for a National
Data Center was, I suppose, similar to that of most
citizens—intense apprehension at the prospects of still
more invasions of personal privacy. In so many areas
technological progress is being secured at the expense of
personal liberty. The projected National Data Center
seems an almost too fitting symbol for that development.*[20]

Invoking the notion of a threat from computers was not
difficult. The committee evoked a series of images which
could play on popular ambivalence toward computers. The
computer is viewed by many both as a miracle worker and as
a ubiquitous evil. The notion of a personal dossier bank with
the overtones of totalitarianism attached thereto raised equally horrendous images. As long as the SSIP members focused
on such symbols, which they did with great skill and persistence, the more technical issues could be and were swept
aside. No probing into technicalities seemed necessary to the
SSIP members when a witness from the Bureau of the Budget
could testify that he saw no way in which information in the
proposed data bank could be stored usefully without some
form of individual identification attached to the data.

The witnesses were chosen to testify in the SSIP hearings largely to demonstrate that the data bank had to be
considered as a policy issue with moral overtones. The function of many of the witnesses was to show that persons with
technical expertise saw the problem in the same light as did

the SSIP members. The complexity of the subject matter, a factor normally limiting the likelihood of oversight, turned out to be no limit at all.

The peripheral relevance of the SSIP's legal authority also emerged in these hearings. Obviously, the facts that a subcommittee such as the SSIP was established and that it had a staff were central to the study. No one seemed to raise the point that although the primary function of the House Government Operations Committee is to promote efficiency and economy in government, here was one of its subcommittees attempting to delay action aimed precisely at improving efficiency and economy. The language in the SSIP report of activities for 1966 makes this point: "Although the subcommittee recognizes that there might be increased economy and efficiency in having centralized statistics at the Government's 'fingertips,' there also would be many dangers."[21]

The major relevance of SSIP relations with the executive branch was their earlier success in altering executive conduct after stimulating public discussion of issues previously considered a matter for technical experts.[22] In matters of executive-legislative relations, as elsewhere, past and present success contributes to future success.

Primary among the opportunity factors were the personal proclivities of the SSIP and of its staff members. This was, after all, a special subcommittee with a precarious existence, one which needed to demonstrate and redemonstrate its reason for being. The SSIP chairman and staff were highly interested in the subject of invasion of privacy, but they were also concerned with justifying their existence. Thus, the SSIP was a subcommittee in search of issues. The data bank proposal seemed to symbolize all of the fears about the loss of privacy in the face of advancing technology.

Conversion factors were important in two ways. First, the Bureau of the Budget's proposal for a new data bank provided the subcommittee with an opportunity that it had been seeking. Second, because the SSIP was operating in a new climate of protest against invasion of privacy, it found avid consumers of its findings in the mass media.

What did the SSIP achieve and how should its achievements be assessed? As noted previously, the SSIP contributed to a major slowdown of the drive to create a data bank and stimulated concern over protection of privacy in establishing the bank. In testimony before the SSIP, Vance Packard asserted:

> I think the Congress and this committee and several other congressional committees have been extremely effective in their roles of alerting, simply by making Federal agency directors aware of the human implications of what they are doing, as, for example, the success which has been achieved in persuading the various departments to make less use of lie detectors and less use of personality testing, the Post Office to stop using the mail cover, the Justice Department to stop using wiretapping, and many agencies to stop using snooper buttons. All these have come about not by legislation but by the mere fact that a body such as yours has explored the situation and made the administrators in the various Federal agencies aware, perhaps for the first time, that there are human values involved. . . . that they have usually responded by establishing safeguards.[23]

Thus, credence is lent to the suggestion that Congressman Gallagher's attempt to "make technologists take account of the broader questions" was at least partially successful.

Writing in January 1968, *New York Times* Washington reporter Nan Robertson could assert that "the idea for the central data bank appears to have run into a wall of hostility, and the biggest reason is Representative Cornelius E. Gallagher of New Jersey."[24]

One concrete result emerged from the SSIP hearings:

the Bureau of the Budget agreed to consult, in building the proposed data bank, not only with its technical experts, but also with social scientists, lawyers, and others concerned with the invasion of privacy. In a speech on August 8, 1967, Mr. Charles Zwick, then assistant director of the Bureau of the Budget, stated:

> *It is the clear intent of the administration to submit a more detailed prospectus of a Data Center to public review and comment before it submits legislation to Congress. This review would include computer scientists, suppliers of information from the business community, and representatives of potential user groups. Assuming a detailed prospectus is evolved and has general support, the administration would then be in a position to submit legislation to Congress.* [25]

One reason the committee could succeed in delaying the national data bank was that its objectives were limited—to amend and to delay, but not to destroy. If the SSIP had set out to kill the proposal for a data bank, no such success could have been predicted.

Personality Tests

The proposal for a national data bank just discussed illustrated how an executive proposal for a new program could stimulate congressional oversight; the case study concerning the use of personality testing in federal employment represented a situation where the impact of particular external events stimulated the SSIP to attempt an oversight effort.

The SSIP held its first public hearings in June 1965. These were designed to cover a variety of issues such as "psychological testing of Federal employees and job applicants, electronic eavesdropping, mail covers, trash snooping, peepholes in Government buildings, the farm census questionnaire, and whether confidentiality is properly guarded in income tax returns and Federal investigative and employment files."[26] Covering all of these topics was the broad umbrella of invasion of privacy.

Although the proposed agenda was somewhat diffuse, some 75 percent of the hearings dealt with only one of these issues—personality testing in federal employment. Other topics were dealt with relatively briefly or simply cast aside. The original subject that brought Congressman Gallagher into public view as a defender of privacy, the use of lie detectors, hovered in the background. One particular incident became a catalyst for Congressman Gallagher. He reported that a seventeen-year-old girl just out of high school "was subjected to humiliating questions about sexual matters when she applied for a job with the National Security Agency as a typist."

With the establishment of the SSIP late in 1964, individuals and groups with complaints about alleged invasions of privacy found an additional outlet for their protests. Letters citing specific problems flooded into Congressman Gallagher's office. Following up on these and other complaints, staff members rapidly discovered a series of issues that seemed to merit further attention.

In his opening statement at the hearings, Congressman Gallagher proclaimed that the purpose of the sessions was "to elicit facts and informed opinion for the record to complete the committee's study of the particular subjects which had been partially developed during the last Congress and to permit the committee to make findings, draw conclusions, and submit recommendations."[27] In reality, as the hearings unfolded, they largely served other functions. Little information emerged that the SSIP members and staff did not already have. The fact-finding function, while salient, was not central.

Substantial evidence suggested that the hearings were not held primarily to generate new information for members of the SSIP. On the basis of previous staff studies and prior consultations with the executive branch, a body of information had already been generated which the hearings did not greatly enhance. Beyond this, several agencies had already reported policy changes to the SSIP which were then "announced" at the hearings.[28]

The major targets of the hearings were top executive branch officials and the interested public. An auxiliary target was Congressman William Dawson, chairman of the Government Operations Committee, to whom the SSIP wished to demonstrate its reason for being.

The two primary oversight functions actually performed were described by a staff member: "To publicize activities relating to invasion of privacy, and to try and get immediate administrative changes in procedures and practices."

The favored method for promoting administrative change was to alert top executive department officials to what technical experts in their own departments and agencies were doing. This information would, it was presumed, facilitate the imposition of tighter political controls over technicians and the injection of more nontechnical values into the decision-making process. "The whole point of my questioning," Congressman Henry Reuss (D.–Wisconsin) suggested to Dr. Al Carp of the Peace Corps, "and the questioning of the Subcommittee has been to urge upon you the greatest care."[29]

A related function was simply to promote sensitivity to the invasion of privacy. As one witness stated: "Your committee . . . has served the function which I think is a very, very valuable function to keep all participants on their toes."[30]

Note the interchange as Representative Frank Horton (R.–New York) questions Mr. Leo Werts, assistant secretary of labor for administration:

MR. HORTON: But the implementation of that policy was one which did permit the so-called personality

*tests, . . . but that when this was called to your atten-
tion, you then made a change in that implementation of
policy because you feel that there is an invasion of the
right of privacy with the use of this type of test; is that
right?*

*MR. WERTS: . . . the supervision of the application of
the policy has been tightened up to the point where this
cannot happen again. . . .*

*MR. HORTON: Do these staff producers [of tests] feel
that these personality tests are not an invasion of privacy? . . .*

*MR. WERTS: Yes, I think they would still say, in their
judgment, these do not constitute invasion of privacy.*[31]

The same point was raised later by Chairman Gallagher:

*Well, I think this goes back to the original point the
chairman made, that while it was not the intention of
the Department to violate the privacy of the individual
concerned—the net effect may well have been just that.
And if this committee can serve any purpose at all, it is
the hope that we can get the technicians together with
the policymakers on this matter and remedy the situation.*[32]

Reviewing the experience of the SSIP, Norman Cornish,
the first chief of inquiry for the SSIP, commented in an
interview:

*Basically the technicians who run the programs in the
executive departments are not anxious to change them.
They would rather go ahead with their own programs,
but the top policy makers are more sympathetic to what
the committee wanted. Many of these top executive
officials have never really thought about the question of
the invasion of privacy previously and had reviewed the*

practices of their departments in terms of this subject matter. They became more sensitive to this issue as a result of the work of this committee.

Beyond helping to accomplish these objectives, the SSIP hearings served as a vehicle for demonstrating committee success in altering administrative behavior. Executive officials, in turn, were allowed to show their responsiveness, in a friendly and congenial atmosphere, to the efforts of the Congress to bring about change. According to a staff member, the design for these performances was carefully drawn: "We tried to stage each of our hearings, to orchestrate them, to arrange them in such a way that the executive department can come in and indicate to us that the problems that we have uncovered no longer exist and that they are taking corrective action."[33] Another SSIP staff member interviewed provided a variation on the same theme:

> *Formal hearings are clearly a threat to the executive departments concerned. To minimize the impact of this threat, the executive agencies acted in many cases very quickly. Staff investigations were held before any particular hearing session. The staff people would identify the problems and present them to the agency officials. The committee had the facts to hang them with and they knew it. After the changes were made, the hearings served the purpose of publicizing this fact. Our chairman called these hearings "our dialogue" with the executive branch.*

It is often difficult to measure the impact of a particular act. The SSIP impact through its study of personality testing in federal employment is of this variety. But several results did emerge clearly. John Macy, chairman of the Civil Service Commission, noted: "You have put the spotlight on it [the problem of personality testing] which is very helpful. It has permitted us to restate our policy in somewhat more definitive terms."[34]

The Peace Corps examined its practices in the area of personality testing:

> *Thanks, really, to being alerted by this committee, we have reviewed our procedures [in the storage of test protocols] and have realized that we can go even further. As of about 2 weeks ago, due to the prompting of this committee, all of these test protocols are being destroyed immediately after they have served their purpose. . . . This [destroying of protocols] was prompted by the inquiry from this committee. It has been a serious mistake for us not to have had a firm policy on this in the past. . . .*
>
> *When this committee first initiated its inquiries into the use of personality inventory tests our initial reaction frankly was to believe that we had already used all these precautions which could be reasonably used to protect against any unnecessary invasion of privacy. Nevertheless, because of your concern and because of your diligence in pursuing that concern, we have carefully reexamined and reconsidered the procedures that we now use. . . . We now have, we believe, a series of procedures by which . . . the privacy of the individual can be better protected.*[35]

Similar examples involving the Office of Education, the Export-Import Bank, the Labor Department, and the Department of the Interior also were developed during these hearings.[36]

The hearings were valuable in drawing publicity and attention. They were widely covered in newspapers and magazines, and Congressman Gallagher was subsequently invited to speak to many organizations about the invasion of privacy. A staff member reported:

> *There is much interest now in invasion of privacy, and much of this can be explained as the result of the work of our committee and those in the Senate. This has become a popular issue now, both in the general sense and the academic communities and specialists in particular. If you look at the* Reader's Guide *several years ago, you would find almost nothing on the invasion of privacy no matter under what headings you looked. Now there are reams of references both in the popular journals and the professional journals. In this sense, Gallagher's subcommittee has accomplished a major function already, and that is simply to bring this issue into the public realm and raise it to the level where experts would look at it explicitly and make it part of the realm of discourse rather than an exotic issue.*

The limits of the SSIP oversight efforts were as clear as is their value. The committee could not undertake and regularly update an agency-by-agency survey. It was impossible for any congressional committee to follow through on the implementation of policy changes on a continuing and systematic basis. The agency-by-agency approach surely required more time and manpower than the SSIP had.

Second, today's victory in a change of policy may be eroded tomorrow by reinterpretation or inaction. Here again the SSIP lacked the resources for adequate follow-through. As Professor Monroe Freedman noted in the hearings: "That policy, just as it was announced in connection with these hearings, could be changed tomorrow and no one would know the difference."[37]

Third, the exact impact of the SSIP on the executive branch's use of personality testing and related invasion-of-privacy questions was difficult to assess because parallel oversight efforts on personality tests were being made about the same time by the Senate Judiciary Subcommittee on Constitutional Rights (SSCR) chaired by Senator Sam Ervin

(D.–North Carolina). Precise credit to a subcommittee was difficult to apportion even if general credit to the Congress was not.

The efforts of these two subcommittees strengthened the congressional hand but also provided some insight as to why the Congress had difficulty in overseeing. The resources available to the Congress were not marshaled to maximize effectiveness. Rather, each committee and subcommittee tended to conduct its operations independently. The following sentences were frequently used by interviewees: "Each House has a life of its own. Each goes its own way." The SSIP and the SSCR, in their handling of the issue of personality testing in the federal government, presented a striking illustration of this phenomenon.

Both subcommittees had exhibited interest in the entire area of invasion of privacy. In the summer of 1964, the staff of the SSCR began an agency-by-agency survey of the uses of personality testing by federal government agencies. Since the SSIP did not come into being until several months later, the Ervin subcommittee apparently got there first. This impression is confirmed by Professor Monroe Freedman, testifying in subsequent SSCR hearings: "This subcommittee is to be commended for being the first congressional committee to recognize the seriousness of psychological testing in Government employment."[38] Yet, early in 1964, Congressman Gallagher was stating to the House of Representatives that a congressional committee should study the problems of invasion of privacy generally.[39]

Whichever subcommittee got there first, by late 1964 both were actively involved in studying the problems of personality testing in federal employment. According to one source, an attempt by staff members from the two units to coordinate activity fizzled after one meeting:

> *They [the subcommittees] tried to resolve their problems in terms of scheduling hearings and so forth by*

*having one staff meeting. It broke up into a debate as to
who got there first, and whose issue it was. It was not
fruitful to continue these discussions because these
problems simply could not be solved. So what happened
was that each committee went its own way and held
hearings from different foci about the same time.*

The House hearings began on June 2 and ran for about
seventeen hours. The Senate hearings began some five days
later, running for about twenty hours. Apparently the jock-
eying for position between the two committees was fierce.
One report has it that the Ervin hearings were announced and
the schedule for the Gallagher hearings was advanced. Writing
in a special issue of the *American Psychologist*, Michael
Amrine asserted: "Newsmen following this business said that
it appeared Representative Gallagher did not want to let this
juicy headline topic come to first attention from the Senate
side of the Capitol."[40]

Thirteen witnesses appeared in the House; fourteen in
the Senate. Four persons testified before both committees.
One department and one interest group sent different spokesmen to testify before the two groups. At least half of the
witnesses covered common ground before the two subcommittees.

Much of the pattern in the Senate followed that in the
House. The hearings were used to allow executive officials
who had been responsive to committee inquiries to announce
changes they had made. Agency representatives were also
allowed to demonstrate how the work of the committee had
stimulated change. With regard to the Peace Corps, Dr. Al
Carp testified: "So we decided not to ask for responses to
those items [on the MMPI tests] which are not scored, . . . as
a result of the studies we have made generated by this
subcommittee."[41] Similarly, Dr. John Macy, chairman of the
Civil Service Commission, reported: "This is a restatement
[of a policy on personality testing] because of the attention

that this subcommittee and the subcommittee in the House have given to this issue."[42]

The reaction to the statement by Chairman Macy illustrates how problems of prestige and competition for publicity between congressional committees intrude into the legislative process. Macy testified before the SSIP on June 3 and read the policy restatement by the Civil Service Commission on Personality Testing. Chairman Gallagher was obviously delighted with the Macy report. "I would like to congratulate you on your statement. . . . this is the first public announcement of this policy."[43] Congressman Rosenthal shared the pleasure of the chairman: "I want to join with the chairman in complimenting you on what I consider rather progressive, forthright views on this subject."[44] The subcommittee members then went on to elaborate on what they saw as a tremendously significant statement by the commission. While Mr. Macy insisted that this was merely a restatement of the previous civil service policy, the SSIP clearly saw it as a new and significant step.

About a week later, Chairman Macy made the same announcement at the hearings of the Ervin subcommittee. The news was essentially stale now. What public attention there was had already gone elsewhere. Senate subcommittee questioners, aware of the same facts as the SSIP, chose to interpret the Macy statement quite differently. The chief counsel and staff director for the Ervin subcommittee, William Creech, commented: "I was under the impression from some of the press reports which were circulated last week that the Commission had actually come up with a new policy. But upon a review of your statement before the committee, it seems quite apparent that there is no new policy."[45] Mr. Macy, of course, was happy to agree. In a highly ambiguous situation such as this one, differences in interpretation will surely arise concerning the meaning of the same act. But note that each subcommittee emphasized the interpretation of the Civil Service Commission's statement that fit its own status and prestige objectives.

An interesting sidelight concerns the differences in style and strategy between the House and Senate subcommittees. Sharply limited in the number of staff members and budget available to it, the SSIP could only press its investigations in the agencies where it had become aware of a problem and where fairly rapid results might be expected. The SSIP wanted substantive results but also the credit for stimulating them. The Senate subcommittee, with a larger and more experienced staff and a much more substantial budget, could proceed more systematically through an agency-by-agency survey.

A second difference emerged in the way the hearings were conducted. While all members of the SSIP participated regularly in the hearings and staff members asked questions after the members themselves finished, the Senate pattern was quite different. Most members of the Senate subcommittee were absent frequently. The chairman asked questions and made comments, but the major thrust came from the committee counsel, who artfully directed the proceedings while deferring the spotlight to the chairman. It was the norm at the Senate hearings for three professional staff members from the staff of the subcommittee to attend. In the House, staff members attending other than the one from the SSIP came from the full Government Operations Committee.

The perceptions of the Senate-House relationships by the legislative participants were revealing of the difficulties that arise. From the perspective of the House members: "We do the work and they get the publicity." Similar statements were made by members of the House Post Office and Civil Service Committee. One staff member closely involved and keenly aware of all of the House-Senate relationships on invasion-of-privacy questions put it this way:

My analysis is this. A congressman does not want to go to a senator. A senator does not normally pay much attention to a congressman. This tends to limit coordination. Questions of credit arise. Something happens. Who or what caused it? Who gets the credit? All congressmen are highly sensitive to publicity. Besides, we do not have enough staff to keep coordinating with them. We have enough staff to barely get our own work done. Besides, once a topic is revealed, Senate subcommittees have large permanent staffs. They can get going on it and take away what we have done. They steal our materials. The Senate committees, with their greater access to publicity, are able to take tremendous advantage of this.

Whether fact, distortion, or paranoia was reflected in this statement may be less important than the fact that many House members and committee staff members felt the same way and seemed to act accordingly.

One inhibiting factor in legislative oversight is that the human and material resources available to the Congress are seldom mustered for coordinated action. On the basis of previous analyses the explanations for this rampant individualism should be apparent: Coordination gaps are largely a function of priorities and interests of the members. Coordination in oversight is largely a function of whether participants find it useful in promoting their own purposes, whatever these might happen to be.

Invasion of privacy was an infant issue for the Congress in 1964–1965. By 1974, it had emerged as an area of substantial concern to many members of Congress and to several committees and subcommittees. The Special Subcommittee on the Invasion of Privacy surely hastened the transition from relative obscurit· to central issue.[46]

Chapter 5 The House Judiciary Committee: Subcommittee Five

Like other standing committees, the House Judiciary Committee is expected to maintain "continuous watchfulness" over the bureaucracy. Chapters 2 through 4 have demonstrated that this legal obligation tells us little about how committees actually behave. The analysis in this chapter confirms this judgment.

Legal Factors

The jurisdiction of the House Judiciary Committee provides an effective challenge for its members. The following list is illustrative of committee responsibilities in 1965–1967: judicial proceedings, constitutional amendments, civil rights, interstate compacts, immigration, apportionment, and presidential succession.

According to its former chairman, Emanuel Celler (D.–New York), some one-third to two-fifths of all House bills are referred to the Judiciary Committee.[1] Its jurisdiction is vast; its legislative load is heavy. The chairman asserts that his is the busiest committee in the House.

The Judiciary Committee was divided into five numbered subcommittees. Subcommittee Five was formally charged with jurisdiction over antitrust, a heavy burden in an increasingly large and complex society where corporate mergers and other combinations seem limited largely by the imagination of the participants. A better explanation for the subcommittee's burdens, however, is that the chairman of the full committee was also chairman of Subcommittee Five, to which he referred items he regarded as important.[2] Congressman Peter Rodino (D.–New Jersey), then ranking majority member on Subcommittee Five, asserted:

> *The major problem is the broad jurisdiction of the subcommittee and the fact that the subcommittee is so busy with legislation. We deal with civil rights; we deal with antitrust; we deal with crime bills, with violence bills, with some aspects of the judicial structure. . . . Our scope is very wide.*

Representative Byron Rogers (D.–Colorado) echoed Rodino's comments and added: "This is a catchall subcommittee used by the chairman for whatever he thinks is appropriate and important. This is, therefore, a very busy legislative committee."

On a committee as active as Judiciary, financial resources can be crucial in stimulating oversight. Chairman Celler saw money as no great problem for the Judiciary Committee: "I don't ask for much, but I always get what I ask for. I am never turned down."

If the chairman is correct, what is asked for still needs to be considered. Some members of Subcommittee Five felt that more money would have been useful for specific investigations. Celler did not request it, they suspected, because he anticipated that his request might not be honored. One member in particular said that he had to use his own money to visit southern communities to see how civil rights legislation was working out. The comments the member received when he did this were indicative of the hostility to requests for funds for such purposes. One congressman told him: "Don't you go into my district if you want to find out anything about it. Ask me and I'll tell you."

The discrepancy between the reports of the chairman and those of at least two members of Subcommittee Five may rest on their perspectives rather than on facts. The two members who cited a need for more funds for the subcommittee had a primary interest in oversight investigations and civil rights. The chairman, while sharing their strong concern with promoting civil rights, had to weigh other factors in deciding whether to seek funds. He may not have been willing to pay the political price for a particular result.

Staff

Chairman Celler did not view staff as a significant opportunity factor: "It's adequate to do our work." If the committee decided to undertake more formal oversight, either by creating a new subcommittee or by altering the mission of one of the existing subcommittees, then more staff might be useful, but, a staff member reported:

If other staff members were added, they would be drawn toward the current activity of the committee. Even if staff members were added for oversight purposes specifically, for example, as recommended by the Joint Committee on the Organization of the Congress, this would not have value simply because that person despite his label as a staff member for oversight would be inevitably drawn into what was going on.

Committee interviewees agreed that more staff was important only if the committee decided to do new things. Ultimately, they argued, members' attitudes and preferences are central: "More staff is not crucial because if we had more staff and they developed some materials, they would still have to come to us to act. We have adequate staff to do what we want to do."

A staff member closely involved in civil rights work for the committee shared this perspective: "The existence of more staff is not a real problem in promoting effective oversight. In the abstract, more staff may always be desirable, but on this subcommittee, there is plenty of staff to handle the problems. The central variable is simply members' time."

An interesting insight about the role of staff in the legislative process emerged from the reflections of a senior staff member who had worked for several judiciary subcommittees, including one dealing with civil rights. He saw the staff role as varying with the subject matter:

> *The subcommittee . . . is a technical committee, and I must educate the members. The members did not know anything when we started. We conducted a technical five-year study. I published a . . . study which has come to be the definitive work in the area. When the members want to know a question, and when they get pressured from interest groups, they come to me and ask what is the situation. What should I do? What are the appropriate responses? In the . . . subcommittee, however, this is hardly the case. The members are keenly aware of the problems and aware of the implications of these problems in their own districts and therefore would never think of coming to staff for judgment. On the . . . subcommittee, oversight is a question of fact-finding, of fact-gathering, establishing what the real world is. The assumption is that there is an objective real world out there and with sufficient diligence we can track it down. This is a response to pressure, but to different pressure than in a civil rights committee area where we are basically evaluating policy. As the result of this we do not use hearings to establish a single factual record but we eventually use the hearings as a ventilation process. This is not simply fact-finding and fact-gathering to establish the reality out there. This is a process of letting the various groups air their views partly because congressmen can argue they are showing the bureaucrats what the constituents think. This is involved then in the congressman's own political life. He is not going to take a tech-*

nical, staff-oriented position in this kind of situation as
he would in terms of the . . . subcommittee.

Thus, again, the role that staff plays in committee activities is
closely conditioned by member desires and priorities.

Subject Matter

Many problems concerning the role of the federal government in policy-making and implementation involve matters of judgment and values more than technical expertise. It
is in such situations that congressmen feel most able to
supervise what the bureaucrats are doing. If the members
want to act on a civil rights issue, the subject matter is not so
technical and complex as to inhibit their efforts severely.

Civil rights issues tend to be highly visible. A member
who sees political gains from activity on civil rights questions
will find a ready audience among newspapermen and other
representatives of the mass media. Members who sought
positions on Subcommittee Five presumably wished to be
near the center of legislative activity on civil rights. The
visibility of the subject matter normally enhances the potential for oversight. However, one staff member saw the
nature of the subject matter as providing a key to understanding the dearth of formal oversight efforts in civil rights:

> *In a sense, the situation in the civil rights area is simply*
> *too dynamic for oversight in the orthodox sense. The*
> *operation in the Justice Department has not become so*
> *bureaucratized that it is possible to look at it and seek*
> *patterns of effective or ineffective activity. There are*
> *simply too many changes occurring, legislatively and*
> *otherwise, for this to take place. Administrative stan-*
> *dards don't exist. Standards change too fast for a con-*
> *gressional committee to be able to look at them very*
> *seriously.*

Committee Structure

The House Judiciary Committee in 1965–1967 had five numbered subcommittees and several special subcommittees. Each numbered subcommittee had a primary jurisdiction and also jurisdiction to receive whatever bills were sent there by the chairman. Representative Celler himself chaired Subcommittee Five because he wanted to handle sensitive issues. Under these circumstances, the hypothesis concerning decentralization and heightened tendencies toward oversight cannot be tested here. In an interview printed early in 1969, Congressman Celler was asked by a newspaper reporter why he insisted on holding the chairmanships of the full committee and also of Subcommittee Five. Celler's reply said it all: "Because I want to control both."[3]

Even those members of the committee, such as Representative Robert Kastenmeier (D.–Wisconsin), who wanted more civil rights oversight, did not feel that the committee's structure was the central inhibiting factor. Kastenmeier proposed a separate oversight subcommittee as an expedient to get "autonomy and funds for investigative personnel." He assumed that an oversight-minded member would chair such a subcommittee.

Committee structure explained less about civil rights oversight by the House Judiciary Committee than did status on the committee.

Committee Status

The chairman of a standing committee always has significant potential power. An astute and forceful person can convert this potential into immense leverage. Emanuel Celler did so. The power of the chairman was demonstrated first in his selecting members to serve on Subcommittee Five. Having anointed the subcommittee to receive crucial items, the chairman then hand-picked its members: "I select the Democrats;

the ranking Republican recommends Republicans and I mostly accept his recommendations."

The chairman's role in full-committee decision-making was equally decisive. According to a ranking majority member of the committee:

> *Ultimately, the subcommittee's conduct is determined by the chairman. In this case, since Congressman Celler is chairman of the full committee as well as chairman of Subcommittee Five, this is pretty much a chairman-run committee. This does not mean that the chairman is dictatorial. This does mean that what the chairman thinks is crucial, goes. The chairman, on many issues when he has either mixed feelings or not any very strong feelings, is perfectly willing to consult, he is always willing to listen to ideas of others. In that sense there is more of a broad context than just the chairman making decisions by himself. On the other hand, when the chairman makes up his mind and really wants something, that is pretty much what goes.*

A highly perceptive minority staff member reinforced this position: "The chairman is in complete control if he wants to be. Representative Celler is a smart chairman. He knows the practical situation and therefore he knows when to give in when he has to. But if he thinks there is a hot issue involved, if he is very concerned with the issue, he will generally get his way. He deliberately sends all hot items to Subcommittee Five."

One factor which the chairman must take into account is the power of the ranking minority member. On civil rights issues, the Judiciary Committee was divided. According to a minority staff member:

> *In 1967 there were fifteen Republicans and twenty Democrats. But of the Democrats, four were southern Democrats who could and would at times go in with the*

Republican minority. So if Representative McCulloch [the ranking Republican member] can hold the Republicans together, which he often can do, and join with the southern Democrats, he can in effect run the committee. Celler needs McCulloch, and Celler knows this. So that if McCulloch takes a strong position on an issue, Celler knows that he has to consider it carefully and often accommodates McCulloch—simply because of the fact that McCulloch could control the committee on some issues of civil rights if he chose to.

Status on this committee also affected Senate-House relationships. When it came to civil rights activity, the House and Senate committees, as in chapters 2 through 4, went their own way. Chairman Celler stated, "There is no cooperation with the Senate committee because we disagree so much. Eastland's position is clear and so is mine."

Relations with the Executive

The political party affiliations of legislators and of the administration were relevant to oversight activity in the Post Office Committee but not in the SSIP. On issues of civil rights, the party affiliations of those who controlled the executive branch and those who ran the Judiciary Committee were seen by congressional participants as being central. "Partisanship is a basic factor in oversight. If the Republicans control the committee, there would be a big difference in the oversight done. This is simply partisanship, not an ideological difference." Another senior majority member carries the point further: "We are of the same party as the president and of course we do not want to do anything to harass the president unless there is something absolutely wrong with the programs." A majority staff member concurs, viewing partisanship as "absolutely vital."

Minority staffers viewed partisanship as more relevant

for civil rights than for many other issues that the committee faced: "Republicans with a Democratic administration generally want more oversight." "If the committee were dominated by Republicans and not by Democrats, it is very likely that there would be a great deal more oversight."

A second aspect of relations with the executive is how the executive branch treats the congressmen. Most members of Judiciary Subcommittee Five felt that they were treated well by the Justice Department. A majority member noted: "I have no trouble in getting information from the Justice Department. We share common ends and are working together. They do not hesitate to give me information." Another senior member cited a personal experience illustrative of his treatment: "I knew a guy down there in the Justice Department who worked pretty well with certain kinds of questions and he left the Justice Department. So I asked the attorney general who to call now. He said, 'You just call me direct whenever you need anything.' This is the kind of cooperation I get."

All of the Subcommittee Five members and staff who were interviewed agreed with this generalization. Similarly, many expressed a high regard for the officials in the executive branch with whom they dealt on civil rights questions. This regard weakened any desire to oversee.

Behind this readiness to please was the executive realization that civil rights questions were always volatile in the Congress and that extensive consultation with congressional leaders was required if programs were to be adopted and implemented successfully.

Intermingled with personal satisfaction with treatment by the executive was policy agreement with the executive. Typically, civil rights legislation over the years had been hammered out in consultation with the House Judiciary Committee. Subcommittee Five, recall, was shaped by Chairman Celler to get a pro—civil rights group. One result was the evolution of a broad policy consensus which promoted executive-legislative harmony, which in turn cooled most passions for oversight. A majority member stated a position articulated by many members: "There is close contact between members of the subcommittee and the Justice Department. We are aware of what they are doing and generally agree with it. We are looking for ways to help the Justice Department do more rather than to investigate what has been done." A staff member reported: "Where there is agreement between the member and a particular executive department, there will not be much of a tendency to oversee unless the member feels that there is somehow political gain in terms of his own performance and record."

The impression quickly emerged that most members of Subcommittee Five, along with key staff people, shared a common conclusion: Oversight was conducted normally not to affect programs that were running satisfactorily, but more often to discover and challenge administrative judgment and error. It was policy conflict that led southern Democrats and others opposed to civil rights legislation to press for investigations. But since these interests had been carefully screened from Subcommittee Five, their impact was to be felt largely in other arenas.

Adding these facts about the relationships with the executive together, it was clear that this opportunity factor provided no great stimulus for Subcommittee Five to oversee.

Member Priorities

An analysis of the seventh opportunity factor, member priorities, revealed why the Judiciary Committee and Subcommittee Five in particular were so active. Unlike the Post Office and Civil Service Committee, whose members often served on other committees that they found more interesting, most of the members of the Judiciary Committee, especially those on Subcommittee Five, had only one committee assignment.[4] Table 5 provides the relevant data. Those who had

TABLE 5: Committee Assignments for Members of Judiciary Subcommittee Five

Member	Committees	Subcommittees	Chairmanships or Ranking Minority Memberships
Democrats			
Celler	1	1	2
Rodino	1	3	0
Rogers	1	2	1
Donohue	1	2	0
Brooks	2	3	1
Kastenmeier	1	3	0
Corman	1	1 (1st sess.)	0
		3 (2d sess.)	
Republicans			
McCulloch	2	4	1
Cramer	2	7	2
Lindsay (1st sess.)	1	3	0
Mathias	2	5	1
McGregor (2d sess.)	1	4	1

Source: Compiled from data in CQ Weekly Report, *April 30, 1965, pt. 1;* CQ Weekly Report, *June 10, 1966, pt. 1.*

more than one committee assignment typically regarded their assignment to Judiciary and especially to Subcommittee Five as their top priority for committee work.[5] "I give almost complete attention to Subcommittee Five, as do many of the other members on it. We regard it as a top-priority committee. We work very hard on it. It gets as much attention as possible."

This high interest in the work of Subcommittee Five was fortified by a perceived norm of the committee: member pride in their output. The chairman commented: "We don't make mistakes; we take great pride in and care in our work." For most members, this was an interesting and worthwhile committee with norms calling for high performance. How did these assets manifest themselves in behavior? The answer was mainly in legislation.

The members of Subcommittee Five saw it essentially as a legislative group. They were satisfied that this perception, when added to the volume of work that the committee received from the House, and the trouble-shooting functions of Subcommittee Five, provided an adequate explanation for why they did not conduct more investigations. Moreover, they saw the burdens of Subcommittee Five as severe because its work was highly controversial as well as important and time consuming. "While the members work very hard on the subcommittee and do give it their primary attention in most cases, there is simply too much legislation which interferes with our other work." "On some committees, you deal with a couple of things and it is all over for the year, and you have time to think about oversight. On this subcommittee it is one thing after another. We don't have the time."

The subcommittee members explained the absence of much formal oversight by citing a lack of time caused by many crucial activities. Others agreed that there was a great deal of truth to this conclusion. Differences arose not over the accuracy of the conclusion but over whether it provided a sufficient explanation.

Careful probing began to uncover other reasons for a dearth of formal oversight. One group of members and staff persons argued that investigations in civil rights were too controversial, that southerners usually did not want them.

> The southerners don't want the committee snooping around trying to investigate things in this area. They don't want any field trips. It is quite understood that the Judiciary Committee and one of its subcommittees could travel to Vietnam to look into refugee problems but could not travel to Richmond to look into civil rights problems. To get the money for such investigations, it would be necessary to go to the Rules Committee, and it is understood that no money would be forthcoming.

*I made a trip on my own to see what was going on in
some of the southern communities. The committee
can't get money for such things and won't be able to
because this involves going into other members' districts and doing some work there that they might be
opposed to.*

Without disputing the accuracy of the central explanation—lack of time—and accepting the conclusion that obtaining funds for formal investigations might not be too easy,
other members placed the emphasis elsewhere: "We are busy,
but we are not that busy that we couldn't schedule some
investigations if we really wanted to badly enough. The fact
of the matter is that the majority does not."

A powerful and adept committee chairman, who was
also chairman of Subcommittee Five and who did not want
to get involved in much formal oversight on civil rights
questions, diminished the likelihood that the subcommittee
would do so. Chairman Celler was not anxious for a systematic review of Justice Department activities. This was
partly because he was intimately involved in creating civil
rights programs and was consulted frequently about their
implementation. In addition, he was simply very busy. Beyond that, he feared that the results of such an investigation
might not help the cause of civil rights: "All civil rights
decisions have to be made by a coalition. An oversight
subcommittee would have to have southern Democrats and
some conservative Republicans on it. I could not get an
all-liberal committee. I don't think that if such an investigation were held that it would be fair."

The chairman argued that the Congress was informally
involved in executive decision-making, that he approved of
executive conduct generally, and that he feared the impact of
a "biased" investigation. Each of these factors goes far toward explaining why Subcommittee Five did not undertake
more formal oversight. These preliminary judgments are ex-

panded and clarified by developing them in three areas: (1) the Kastenmeier proposal for an oversight committee; (2) the school guidelines investigations in 1966; and (3) oversight accomplished during legislative hearings.

An Oversight Committee?

Representative Robert Kastenmeier, a member of the House Judiciary Committee and of Subcommittee Five, was a vocal advocate of a special constitutional rights subcommittee to deal with questions of individual rights and constitutional guarantees. He was concerned especially with the implementation of the Voting Rights Act of 1965. This led the representative from Wisconsin to propose in a letter to Chairman Celler, dated September 28, 1965, that a special voting rights subcommittee be created. Kastenmeier and others wanted an institutionalized mechanism in the Congress for overseeing the implementation of the civil rights bills passed since 1957.

Following a complicated set of negotiations, a special ad hoc advisory committee on civil rights which was to report to Subcommittee Five emerged in October 1966. The three members were Representative Kastenmeier, chairman, Representative James Corman (D.–California), and Representative Charles Mathias (R.–Maryland). Each was concerned with the effectiveness of civil rights legislation as well as with its consequences.

The ad hoc committee had three formal purposes: to evaluate compliance with the Civil Rights Acts of 1957, 1960, and 1964, and with the Voting Rights Act of 1965; to assess the desirability of establishing an oversight committee; and to establish whether the power to conduct field investigations and to subpoena witnesses would be desirable. According to one committee member, "We were not encouraged to hold hearings." Twenty-eight informal conferences were held over six days with federal officials, with spokesmen for interested groups, and with officials from southern states. Eighteen officials from several executive departments participated, as did thirteen persons from a variety of interested groups and five officials from southern states. In addition, four southern state officials submitted written statements for the record. Thirteen others were unable to appear.[6]

According to one staff member, no verbatim records were kept. Most of the testimony centered around Title VI of the 1964 Civil Rights Act, which provided for the withholding of federal funds under specified circumstances. Representative Kastenmeier asserted that "throughout the conferences, it was the opinion of all parties that an oversight committee be established within the Judiciary Committee."[7]

The ad hoc committee presented its report to Subcommittee Five in February 1966 and then disbanded. The report was not published as a committee print; instead, Representative Kastenmeier inserted it in the *Congressional Record* on September 21, 1966, during debate on an attempt by the Rules Committee to wrest the oversight function in civil rights from the Judiciary Committee.[8] The ad hoc committee made four recommendations:

First. *That a subcommittee, existing or special, within the House Judiciary Committee be authorized and directed to attend to matters involving voting and civil rights on a continuing basis.*

Second. *That such subcommittee be authorized to travel within the continental limits of the United States for the purpose of conducting appropriate on-site hearings and/or investigations.*

Third. *That adequate funds for professional staff and for other purposes be obtained for such subcommittee.*

Fourth. *That authority to require the attendance of such witnesses and the production of such books or papers or other documents or vouchers by subpoena or otherwise be obtained for such subcommittee.*[9]

The central recommendation was that a specific subcommittee for oversight in civil rights be established. The assumption underlying this proposal was the need for an *autonomous* group with a precise mission if effective oversight was to be achieved.

Chairman Celler did not grant these requests himself. He had been known to do similar things in the past, but in this case he referred the matter to the full committee, where it more or less died. One staff member, attempting to explain the absence of a positive committee reaction, stressed the pressures of other business. Many observers were convinced that this explanation provided less than the whole story.

Why did these efforts fail despite the support of members who shared the chairman's views on civil rights questions and who earnestly were seeking progress? The principal reason seemed to lie in a set of complex judgments about political efficacy. Chairman Celler, and apparently enough other members to kill the proposal, had seemingly reached two conclusions. First, however desirable more formal oversight might seem to be as an aid to the cause of civil rights, in fact, the net impact would probably not be more effective enforcement, but more pressure for less enforcement. Second, sufficient oversight was being carried on through other, less formal means.

The first proposition was to be tested shortly in the controversy over federally imposed school guidelines. The second suggestion can be probed by looking at the relationships between oversight and legislation, as well as by recalling the feeling among senior majority members of Subcommittee Five that they had excellent contacts and rapport with the Justice Department and other federal agencies involved in civil rights enforcement.

School Guidelines

The controversy over the implementation of the guidelines for school desegregation illustrates how formal oversight can be stimulated (coerced?) into being, even in the face of a reluctant committee or subcommittee. If internal committee pressures for oversight did not move Chairman Celler, external pressures could and did.

In 1964, the Congress passed the Civil Rights Act, Title VI of which permitted the Office of Education to cut off federal funds from programs which discriminated on the basis of race. Section 601 of the act stated: "No person in the United States shall, on the ground of race, color, or national origin, be excluded from participation in, be denied the benefits of, or be subjected to discrimination under any program or activity receiving Federal financial assistance." [10] To implement this provision, section 602 required that:

> *Each Federal department and agency which is empowered to extend Federal financial assistance to any program or activity, by way of grant, loan, or contract other than a contract of insurance or guarantee, is authorized and directed to effectuate the provisions of section 601 with respect to such program or activity by issuing rules, regulations, or orders of general applicability which shall be consistent with achievement with the objectives of the statute authorizing the financial assistance in connection with which the action is taken. No such rule, regulation, or order shall become effective unless and until approved by the President.* [11]

For advocates of school integration, these provisions provided sanctions to promote the law of the land. To segregationists, they meant more federal interference with local autonomy.

As the Office of Education moved to implement this statute, it received pleas for additional guidance from southern school districts. "In response to these repeated and urgent requests by school officials and to get the desegregation program going the Office of Education drew up its first statement of policies or 'guidelines' as they have come to be known, in the spring of 1965."[12]

After modest activity under the statute and guidelines, the Office of Education issued revised guidelines, somewhat more strict, in March 1966. Direct reaction from many southern areas was substantial; indirect reaction through southern congressmen was real and slashing. Enforcement of the guidelines was to become an issue in the passage of the Elementary and Secondary Education Amendments of 1967 when Secretary of Health, Education, and Welfare John Gardner was "forced" into a statement about adequate warnings before final cutoffs of funds as part of the price for the passage of the bill.

In this context of clamor for repeal or modification of Title VI, the demand for oversight intensified. The House Rules Committee on September 29 and 30 and October 4, 1966, held hearings on House Resolution 826, calling for the establishment of a select committee to investigate school guidelines and policies of the commissioner of education in school desegregation.

Chairman Celler of the Judiciary Committee, not previously enamored with oversight in this area, now promised the Rules Committee that the Judiciary Committee would hold a full and fair investigation. Unveiled before the Rules Committee was the Kastenmeier subcommittee, whose report had not even been printed by the Judiciary Committee previously. Chairman Celler, who had received the Kastenmeier report with less than total enthusiasm, now latched onto it and used it as evidence of what the Judiciary Committee could and would do.[13]

Representative William McCulloch (R.–Ohio), the ranking minority member on the Judiciary Committee, in testimony before the Rules Committee, cited the heavy workload of the Judiciary Committee in 1966 and added: "There just was not enough time to implement that [sic] [Kastenmeier subcommittee] recommendations."[14]

The Rules Committee agreed to create the select committee provided for in Resolution 826. Chairman Celler, in a set of Byzantine negotiations, then promised the creation of a special judiciary subcommittee on civil rights if the Rules Committee, in exchange, would not implement House Resolution 826.

Thus, Chairman Celler created the Subcommittee on Civil Rights in November 1966. Hearings followed quickly in December. These happenings, somewhat bizarre in the context of previous committee behavior, were rather simply explained by committee members: "We were sort of pushed into it. We were forced into it. We might have lost our jurisdiction if we didn't." The dual threat of a loss of jurisdiction and of the creation of a select committee not likely to be favorable to desegregation had moved the Judiciary Committee when internal pressures could not.

Three days of hearings designed to relieve the pressure for a full investigation were dominated by the testimony of Harold Howe, commissioner of education. Representatives Kastenmeier and Corman asked searching but essentially supportive questions. Representatives William Cramer (R.–Florida) and Robert Ashmore (D.–South Carolina) attempted to impale the commissioner.

No report emerged from these hearings because, as its chairman, Representative Byron Rogers, succinctly put it, "None is needed." In the 90th Congress, 1967, this special subcommittee was reconstituted as the School Guidelines Subcommittee. In reality, its jurisdiction was civil rights. Reconstitution occurred because as part of the "Treaty of September of 1966," Chairman Celler had promised Chairman Howard Smith (D.–Virginia) of the Rules Committee that southerners could call witnesses. The lengthy interrogation of Commissioner Howe in December had prevented this.

No hearings were held by this special subcommittee in 1967. Chairman Rogers, with a notable lack of enthusiasm, asserted: "We will probably hold some hearings in this session. If we go into anything, it will probably be school guidelines." One staff member commented later: "The chairman is not particularly enthusiastic about having more hearings."

With the immediate pressure lessened and attention shifting elsewhere, the school guidelines subcommittee faded away with barely a whimper. The explanations can be found in the earlier discussion of opportunity factors. Like other organizations, the Congress and its committees do not do what their leadership does not want them to do except in the face of intense, immediate, and sustained external pressure.

A picture has emerged of a committee and a subcommittee essentially uninvolved in oversight in civil rights. Even the one case of actual oversight hearings showed merely that a strong chairman needed to be responsive at times to external pressures. But Subcommittee Five was an active, prestigious committee, so one would have expected to find more concern with implementation there.

Such concern was manifested through informal contacts during the time period studied. Relations between the committee and the Justice Department were close, continuing, warm. Members of the subcommittee generally, and Chairman Celler in particular, undoubtedly had an impact on bureaucratic behavior through these informal contacts and discussions. Subcommittee Five members saw themselves as providing some oversight in this way.

Oversight and Legislative Hearings

The activities described so far suggest that Subcommittee Five was active and interested in civil rights but not in formal oversight. The impact of this conclusion is somewhat blunted as the committee legislative record is scrutinized. In the course of hearings on legislation, Subcommittee Five gave attention to oversight which was less than systematic investigation but more than is involved in routine casework for individuals. Subcommittee Five gave some attention to problems of implementation, though not in a routinized, thorough fashion.

The idea to be probed is that in the course of holding hearings on new legislation dealing with civil rights questions, Subcommittee Five performed considerable oversight but performed it as a latent function.

Most subcommittee members and staff persons asserted that this was the case: "We achieve much oversight as we consider legislation. Hearings for legislation are the major instrument for performance of the oversight function on this subcommittee." But others on the committee saw the formal distinction between legislation and oversight as an accurate reflection of behavior: "Our big question is legislation. This is what we spend our time on. We are not primarily an oversight committee." "The Congress hears too little of the widespread activities undertaken under these statutes. Most pertinent data on civil rights are presented in hearings on the current year's proposals."

How much oversight goes on in legislative hearings can only be determined by an examination of the record of these hearings. Perhaps the committee's self-image as a legislative group rather than as an investigative-oversight committee may reflect a distinction which is more formal than functional.

The legislative hearings held in March, April, and May of 1959, which served as the basis for the Civil Rights Act of 1960, were examined closely in an attempt to discover whether an oversight function was being performed. Formal content analysis did not seem to be warranted for these modest purposes. The hearings were read, and each item relating to oversight was noted and roughly categorized. The seemingly incidental and the trivial were omitted. Such a tabulation revealed some forty examples of more than casual probing concerning oversight matters.[15] The questions fell mainly into three categories: information-seeking, probing for alleged shortcomings in executive action on civil rights matters, and questions about the adequacy of existing funds, personnel, legal powers, and administrative structure.

The questions about alleged shortcomings fell in about equal numbers into two groups: one half suggested the need for more activity while the other half stressed overzealousness in executive implementation of civil rights legislation.

These data fail to support firm conclusions, but they do suggest several inferences.

1. Most of the hearings were not directed to questions and problems about oversight but to building a record, receiving formal statements, and allowing various interests to present their views. Quantitatively, it is difficult to argue that a concern with oversight dominated these sessions.

2. The topics most frequently discussed came up because the executive proposed a new policy and witnesses commented on it. Executive action stimulated legislative attention, but the executive agenda structured much of the ensuing discourse.

3. Congressional questioning focused on discrete issues. Some questions seemed important and others seemed trivial, but there was seldom evidence of substantial or *systematic* inquiry into general problems. Some of the questions did reveal, however, a great deal of previous attention by members and staff to the work of the executive branch on civil rights questions.

4. Alleged failings received more attention than did administrative successes. In all cases, discussion revolved about particular actions or inactions, not about the more general problems which these incidents illustrated.

5. At times, members did use these hearings to gather basic information that they apparently were not aware of previously.

6. When witnesses and members conversed about questions concerning oversight, the dialogue seemed almost rehearsed. Members apparently knew the answers before they

asked the questions. Witnesses were led into confirming members' judgments: "Wouldn't you say that . . ." provided the standard lead-in.

7. More attention was devoted to identifying perceived problems than to intensive discussion and analysis of these problems.

8. As is frequently the case on issues with high emotional quotients, seekers of the ludicrous, the bizarre, the warped, and the trivial could readily satisfy their curiosity in these hearings.

Looking back at these cases, the record became clear. Despite the vigor and activity of the House Judiciary Committee in several important areas of public policy, the committee did not engage in much formal oversight on civil rights issues from 1965 to 1967. Oversight was performed to some unknown extent through informal contacts and latently through legislative hearings. What was still missing, though, was continuous, detailed, systematic inspection of how the civil rights laws had worked out. This omission was no accident but rather the result of a careful, deliberate weighing of political priorities by those who controlled Subcommittee Five, particularly by Chairman Emanuel Celler.

A Postscript

In February 1971, Chairman Celler assigned jurisdiction for civil rights oversight to Subcommittee Four. What accounted for a type of action that had been rejected previously? The answer was to be found in new situations and circumstances. The flood of civil rights legislation beginning in 1957 had ended. A Republican administration perceived by Celler as eroding civil rights legislation previously passed was now in office. Celler's personal influence in the Justice Department had diminished.

In 1973, with a new committee chairman, these factors continued to prevail. When the Judiciary Committee ended its long-standing practice of having numbered subcommittees, one of the new units created was the Subcommittee on Civil Rights and Constitutional Rights.

The same factors which explained committee oversight behavior in 1965–1967 continued to do so. Committee behavior was different because these same factors combined in different ways.

Chapter 6 Oversight as a Latent and a Manifest Function

Chapters 2 through 5 focused on the oversight activities of several committees and subcommittees. Chapter 6 views oversight when performed as a latent function in legislative hearings and in casework. The use of formal reporting procedures to promote oversight is considered also. Things are not always what they seem. Substantial oversight is performed when apparently that is not the case. What is intended is not always achieved; what is achieved may not be what is intended.

Legislative Hearings

The classic image of what legislative hearings do states that "their most important function has been to collect facts so as to enable committee members to make informed judgments regarding legislative proposals."[1] The stress on fact-finding and legislation ignores other functions performed in these sessions. As in the television slogan "All I want are the facts," hearings have been viewed as somewhat apart from the political process. Fortunately, some myths do not die hard. Partly as a result of the research of Ralph K. Huitt, it is now widely understood that the legislative hearing is integral to the political process.

Two recent textbooks on the legislative process reflect this newer view:

Because committee members are not merely neutral judges, they sometimes use the hearings for another purpose, to develop support for, or opposition to, a bill. The Chairman may accomplish this purpose by the timing of the hearings, the selection and priority of witnesses, and the use made of staff resources during the hearing. Other members may use friendly or hostile questions to witnesses in order to achieve the same end. The purpose of these maneuvers may be the narrow one of persuading undecided committee members, or it may be the broader one of generating public interest and support or to impress Congress as a whole.[2]

A second major textbook discusses hearings as follows:

If the principal purpose of hearings were to transmit information to committee members, the major groups would make better use of expert staff personnel as witnesses, because they are better equipped to testify on technical points. The fact is that organizations tend to use . . . their most distinctive members as spokesmen, men whose names command committee respect and newspaper print. . . . The propaganda function is achieved through coverage by the news media, including television and motion pictures.

The traditional interpretation described the committee member as an impartial judge, charged with studying the facts, listening, weighing the evidence submitted by contesting parties, and deciding the case. The committee member's standards, so this interpretation held, were those of the "public interest" and his role was that of guardian. A much newer generalization has it that the member himself may be a willing and active participant in the political struggle, with interests far from neutral.[3]

Awareness of the political essence of hearings is also reflected in the increasing sophistication of newspaper accounts.[4] But this sophistication has not created heightened sensitivity to the utility of hearings for legislative oversight of the bureaucracy. Legislators themselves express difficulty in articulating the relationships between legislation and oversight, much less between hearings and oversight. A typical legislative response to questions about oversight is, "We are a legislative committee." Legislation and procedures connected with it are thought of as separate and distinct from performing oversight. The legislator typically links oversight and investigations. He usually does not associate it with legislative hearings.

Analysis of the case studies of committees and subcommittees in chapters 2 through 5 suggests that the dual linkages—legislation-hearings, oversight-investigations—represent an artificial dichotomy. Functionally, oversight is performed in hearings just as legislation may be linked to investigations. Form and fact may be quite different.

Perhaps the most obvious examples of how hearings relate to oversight are found in the work of the appropriations committees and subcommittees. Ostensibly concerned with enacting appropriation bills, these units spend considerable time probing into what the executive departments have been doing with the money given them the previous year. For example, note the following interchange between Subcommittee Chairman Tom Steed (D.–Oklahoma) and Assistant Postmaster General Tyler Abell during the appropriation hearings for fiscal 1967:

> *MR. STEED. When I joined this committee I had a pet peeve and I have been very pleased either because they were going to anyhow, or because of something I said, that the Department adopted the policy of building Post Offices where the lobby had a street level entrance in-*

*stead of some complicated stairway or something of
that sort. Are you really following that policy?*

MR. ABELL. *I think this is generally an architectural
policy these days. As in all office buildings, you do not
walk up steps anymore except to the Capitol.*

MR. STEED. *It got here before we did. I think the public reacts more favorably to that one thing than probably anything else that Post Office construction has
done in modern times. A Post Office is a building that
sooner or later everybody in the community goes into,
and just like a commercial enterprise it ought to be the
easiest building in town to get into and not the most
difficult.*

MR. ABELL. *As far as I know, it is being done.*

MR. STEED. *It comes home to me because many years
ago, when they built the monstrosity they call a Post
Office in my home town, it had steps and when we re-
modelled it, they were eliminated. I think you can't find
a community on earth that is happier about it than the
patrons of the Post Office in my home town. They had
to endure this monstrosity for so many years. I think
they are no different than people anywhere else. No
commercial enterprise in the world would indulge in
that, and I don't think the federal government ought to
either.*[5]

The issues raised may involve the minute and mundane;
nonetheless, oversight is being performed.

Oversight sometimes develops in peculiar ways. Quite
often in legislative hearings a member will interrupt a witness
with questions or comments seemingly unrelated to the testimony being given. Yet in these forays, members do articulate
problems that they perceive in bureaucratic behavior. The

following statement by Representative Silvio Conte (R.–Massachusetts) is illustrative:

> *MR. CONTE. Mr. Chairman, I realize, General, you have a committee set up to recommend commemorative stamps. However, I would like to make one suggestion for the record. I remember several years ago I made the suggestion to General Day and he was very effective with the committee with regard to the commemorative stamp for the nurses. I had somewhat of a personal interest, my wife being one, you have had one for Girl Scouts and Boy Scouts, and they have been excellent. Norman Rockwell, world renowned artist from my district did the Boy Scout stamp, which was one of the best I have ever seen.*
>
> *Mr. Postmaster General, 1965 marks the twentieth anniversary of the founding of the Girls Club of America.*
>
> *In the years since its founding in 1945, great social strides have been made by this organization. Their leaders are hard-working, dedicated members of our own communities. The Girls Clubs of America are performing invaluable services in guiding our young ladies to lead good, useful lives. These young people of today will be our leaders of tomorrow and I can think of nothing more fitting than to issue a commemorative stamp in honor of this organization. While I fully realize the many requests you have received this year for commemorative stamps, I request that serious consideration be given the issuance of a stamp honoring the Girls Clubs of America.*[6]

The anticipation of these forays into the unknown may strike fear or at least promote anxiety in witnesses. A top Post Office official asserted: "You can't tell a congressman he's being irrelevant." Most comments on congressional interjection of "irrelevancies" into hearings deplore such behavior or curse the possibility of it. This viewpoint ignores the fact that the congressmen seize whatever occasion they can to press points that *they* think require attention.

Avoiding personal discomfort for the bureaucratic witness is seldom a top priority for congressmen. Witness the report of an interchange between Senator Russell Long (D.−Louisiana) and Secretary of Health, Education, and Welfare John Gardner:

> *The major purpose of the hearings [for the Senate Finance Committee] was to allow Mr. Gardner to explain why he ordered in January, a cut off of federal welfare funds to Alabama. Midway in the hearings, however, Senator Long, the committee Chairman, swerved from the subject of welfare to criticize the Civil Rights Commission's report. . . . Senator Long accused the Commission of seeking "racial mixing for mixing's sake" and asked Mr. Gardner whether he shared the Commission's point of view?*[7]

What is functional for the witness and for the consideration of the legislation under discussion may not be functional for the purposes of individual members of the Congress as they seek to oversee. Oversight is being performed whatever the label attached to the proceedings. There is no logic which demands that when members interrupt the testimony of witnesses to interrogate them, the items discussed be either weighty or perceived as relevant by the witness. Of immediate concern at this point in the analysis is the presence of oversight activity. The quality of its performance raises an additional set of questions.

Despite a plethora of such examples, very few legislators or staff members interviewed sensed the relationships between legislation and oversight. Congressman David Henderson (D.−North Carolina) was one of the exceptions. He noted: "I don't separate legislation from oversight; in fact they are inexorably linked."

The Utility of Hearings for Oversight

It is not difficult to establish that oversight occurs during legislative hearings. More complicated is the question of what utility hearings have in promoting oversight. Most interviewees asserted that hearings were mainly window-dressing.[8] Many sharply qualified their generalizations in ways that have received insignificant recognition in the literature on the Congress.[9]

For many members, the utility of the legislative hearing was that it provided a means of seizing a member's time and attention for a particular issue. Even if the hearings were infrequently attended and even if it was necessary sometimes to persuade members to come, those who did attend found that attention was diverted temporarily from casework or other matters to focus on the question at hand. According to one member: "Hearings focus the member's attention. A specific obligation to attend pulls him toward the subject matter." Or, in the words of a staff member in the Senate:

> *A formal hearing is a way of focusing the time and attention of senators. Senators are concerned with reelection, with making a good record, and with promoting the public policy ends that they desire. In the course of such concerns, many pressures compete for their time and energy. A hearing is a way of focusing their time because they either attend or read a summary, or keep up in some way and therefore become concerned with an issue in more depth than might be true otherwise.*

Their interest piqued, members will sometimes probe further into an issue.

Beyond capturing their time, hearings provide a seldom discussed additional advantage for the members. Most congressmen tend to be more people-oriented than thing-oriented. Recruitment and selection processes favor those who move readily among people, those who can communicate easily on a person-to-person basis. The individual who prefers seclusion, whose personal values place a premium on isolation for contemplation, is less often found in the Congress. Many of the skills that get the candidate into office and enable him to stay there are verbal. Most members by habit and by inclination prefer to learn from oral interchange than from lonely reading sessions.[10] The hearings provide such an opportunity. In the words of a senior committee staff member: "Hearings give the members a chance to hear, not read. Many members prefer testimony, prefer listening to oral interchange."

For junior members of a committee, the hearings may provide a relatively painless introduction into the work of the committee. It may build subject matter competence and hence promote subsequent activity and interest. Almost all the junior committee members interviewed cited this aspect of hearings as being important to them.

Many members not on a given committee have only nominal competence in a committee's subject area. The hearing record can educate them or their staffs. At times, the record promotes subsequent staff activity and interest. It is true, however, that most often the records of committee hearings are not read by most other members. When they are, however, they can serve this function.[11]

Hearings also provide a testing ground on which bureaucrats can build or lessen their standing with members of the committee. As hypothesized in chapter 1, a conditioning factor in stimulating or inhibiting oversight is the member's assessment of bureaucrats. The hearings become a useful forum for such assessment. As J. Leiper Freeman notes:

> *Yet often the most vital factors in communications in*
> *committee hearings, as in other small-group assemblages,*

are the methods and the disposition of the communicator plus his listeners' attitudes toward him and what he symbolizes, rather than the alleged facts presented and the logic used.

. . . His [the bureau leader's] influence with the committee may depend not so much upon what he says as upon the impression the committee members form of him as a communicator and as a bureaucrat.[12]

In oversight activities, the presence of formal hearings or of a formal investigation sometimes provides a clue to the breakdown of informal attempts to influence executive behavior. In the interviews, almost all of the congressmen expressed an initial preference for informal discussion. Only two interviewees saw the formal hearing or investigation as the best way to proceed initially in overseeing the bureaucracy: "Hearings are best because a formal record is made. It's harder to evade questions then." "When I sit down and talk things out with people in the executive departments there is no record to be referred to. Public hearings are important to make the record, to provide information for the rest of the Congress."

For most members, formal hearings were a second choice; the necessity to hold a formal hearing was an indicator that informal procedures were not working well.[13] The informal was preferred where the congressmen had ready means of access to the executive branch; the formal was preferred when the informal was not productive.

One senior staff member for a committee reported that he presented evidence of shortcomings in behavior to the executive agency involved in the hope that the errors would be corrected. If not, then the possibility, or perhaps the threat, of a formal hearing lurked in the background. The threat of a hearing is part of the executive-legislative bargaining process, as is the introduction of a bill. Examples are plentiful of bills being introduced as a threat more than with the intent of enacting them. A staff director stated: "The executive gets delirium tremens with the mere mention of a public hearing. They see the formal hearing as a threat to their activity."[14] Or, as one committee chairman put it: "I do not have to use hearings as a formal threat because the executive already knows that the threat exists. This is usually just understood. It seldom has to be discussed explicitly."

The staff director of a subcommittee makes a distinction between top-level bureaucrats and their subordinates:

The attitude of the executive toward oversight tends to be apprehension. It varies with the people involved. Liaison people tend to expect oversight as do people at the top levels of government. Down in the ranks, legislative oversight, or the possibility of it, can have a tremendous impact. The threat of an inquiry is itself an important tool of legislative oversight. It can be a basic tool in dealing with those down in the ranks.

The legislative hearing provides a potentially useful forum for oversight activity. If that potential is not regularly and systematically developed, or if it is not exploited fully, it still remains there to be seized by those who are inclined to do so. Most hearings are not used heavily for oversight purposes.[15] The data cited in chapter 5 support this judgment. Legislative hearings, if not central to oversight efforts, are part of them. Their relevance, such as it is, deserves greater attention.

Legislative Casework

Perhaps the dominant view of legislative casework is a negative one involving symbols such as illicit interference and errand-running.[16] Casework is commonly viewed as involving the trivial, the onerous, the burdensome, and the time-consuming. These ideas are central to the thinking of several congressmen as quoted by Charles Clapp: "I thought I was going to be Daniel Webster and I found that most of my work consisted of personal work for constituents." "This life consists of preoccupation with the unimportant at the expense of the more important." "The least appealing aspect of my job is the service we have to perform for constituents." [17]

In a sample of eighty-seven members in the 88th Congress, Davidson, Kovenock, and O'Leary found that 57 percent of the respondents saw service for constituents as a complaint-problem; that is, as a problem "that prevented him from carrying out the role that he would like to play in the House . . . that prevented the House operating as he thought it should." [18] Among fourteen areas for complaint, this one was exceeded only by the lack of information and the complexity of decision-making.

Alongside this dominant stream of analysis is a secondary line which recognizes the possible importance of casework for reasons other than promoting the likelihood of reelection. Casework is defended for its "humanizing" impact on relations between citizens and bureaucrats[19] and the sense of satisfaction created among congressmen:

> *A Senator can set a business back on its feet, saving a whole town from being parched of its only payroll. Sometimes, by a telephone call with muscle in it, he can see that personal justice is done and change the whole course of a family's life. . . . being able to do that sort of thing brings one of the greatest inner rewards of public service.* [20]

For those who view it positively, casework is sometimes seen as a central function of the Congress:

> *The service function, far from being a time-consuming diversion from the essential legislative duties of members, is central to all of the work of the Congress.* [21]

> *The very knowledge by executive officials that some Congressman is sure to look into a matter affecting his*

constituents acts as a healthy check against bureaucratic indifference or arrogance.[22]

Through the liaison he is called on to perform for his constituents, a member is constantly testing the various agencies of the Federal Government for thoroughness, fairness and efficiency. In my experience their score on all three counts has been consistently high. However, errors of judgment can, and frequently do occur. The challenges that come from the Congressman's constituents undoubtedly contribute much toward keeping the agencies on their toes. The inquiries and exchanges prompted by the complaints from constituents also serve importantly to widen a Congressman's familiarity with the actual workings of the government. When appropriating funds for the annual budgets of the various agencies, those that have demonstrated efficiency are remembered as well as those who have demonstrated otherwise.[23]

With few exceptions, these comments, whether derogatory or in praise, were based on personal experience, on very limited data, or on speculation. Writing in 1966, Walter Gellhorn reported his experience in sampling the mail of ten members of the House of Representatives. In presenting his results, Gellhorn suggested: "The composite result of this investigation is presented without any assertion that it proves exactly what constituents' case work involves for every member of Congress. It is offered for lack of anything better. 'Hard statistics' concerning the quantity or kinds of case work do not exist."[24]

Most congressmen perceived casework as intimately related to political survival. More controversial is what else casework accomplished. In particular, what are the relationships between casework and legislative oversight? On the basis of comments by congressmen in the literature,[25] as reinforced by my own interviews, few congressmen or members of their staffs saw oversight as the primary result of casework. In most instances, service was related simply to survival. In the words of a veteran caseworker with extensive experience in three congressional offices:

> *A third of the offices probably give personal attention to casework beyond just handling the immediate question and keep track of what goes on and what doesn't go on in terms of patterns, and many do not. Many are just handled on a routine basis without any regard for political problems that emerge, simply with regard to handling the cases.*

The typical congressman perhaps uses forms similar to those used by Representative Arnold Olsen for handling routine requests:

Congress of the United States
House of Representatives
Washington, D.C.

Respectfully referred to:

for such consideration and investigation as the communication herewith submitted may warrant. A report, in duplicate, to accompany return of the enclosure will be appreciated.

The Consequences of Casework for Oversight

The congressmen and their staffs viewed casework mainly in terms of individual service; committee staff members were more likely to be concerned with the broad policy implications of the case. It is not unusual for members to seek help on cases from the relevant committee. According to committee staffers, the flood was greater sometimes than they could handle. A committee may be more interested in what the case symbolizes than in the case itself.

Oversight resulting from casework was performed as a latent function rather than as a manifest one. The relationship was clear and consequential, but secondary. What, then, were these consequences for oversight of casework?

These consequences fell into two groups: direct and indirect. The indirect consequences involve various forms of heightened awareness of executive operations. This awareness was a precondition for oversight activities.

The first and most indirect consequence of casework for oversight was that members gained some appreciation of, and information about, certain bureaucratic operations. The cases from which the member became well informed were few, but he did develop an awareness about bureaucratic operations from these day-to-day, routine interactions. This conclusion, based on interviews and inspection of the public record in three areas of domestic policy, was supported by James Robinson in a study conducted on the 86th Congress: "The constituent's inquiry sometimes stimulates the Congressman's interest in foreign policy, and although many so-called 'service requests' are routine, some are not and possess potential policy implications."[26]

Beyond gaining a general sense of operations and general information, congressmen became aware of certain deficiencies in policy implementation. Senator Jacob Javits (R.–New York) in 1968 attempted to influence military policy on the calling up of Air Force units after complaints were received about alleged violations of the Defense Act of 1966.

In a speech on the floor, arguing against the possible closing of some Veterans Administration hospitals, Representative Dulski used constituent complaints about a waiting list for admission to these facilities as evidence of a continuing need.[27]

Multiplying examples is not the same as proof, yet interviews and inspection of the record revealed that the progression from casework to awareness of problems to action was a standard subpattern in congressional behavior. Heightened awareness of possible bureaucratic error was no guarantee that members of the Congress would do anything about the situation, but action was more likely once such awareness did develop.

Interactions coming from casework provide many circumstances under which congressional attitudes toward bureaucrats can be developed. Little hard evidence bearing directly and systematically on the relationship between attitudes and oversight exists. Perhaps the most closely related evidence comes from the research of James Robinson which posits a relationship between congressional attitudes toward a department and departmental performance of the service function, and congressional behavior as concerns that department. Two of his findings are pertinent in this regard:

> *That no statistical relation exists between these two variables [satisfaction with departmental handling of service requests and congressional policy support] is not the same as saying that the Department's attention to Congressional "service" requests does not affect the Department's position with Congress. Our data certainly will not allow us to say that all other things being equal, State's policies would receive the same support if the Department discontinued this function. . . . If the Department were inefficient, unresponsive, or tardy in meeting Congressmen's requests for assistance, Congress would have another ground on which to criticize the Department.[28]*

> *The Department operates on the assumption that the more satisfactorily it handles constituent-initiated requests, the more likely it is to obtain the support of members on policy.[29]*

The linkages between satisfaction and proclivity toward oversight are central here. If possible dissatisfaction is a factor toward promoting oversight, then casework handled well may not prevent oversight but may contribute to lessening the likelihood of its occurring.

A fourth indirect consequence of casework for oversight resulted when a congressman acquired a reputation for concern with particular fields of administrative activity. Having acted on the basis of constituent complaints and having publicized his actions, the member might well advance his potential and capacity for conducting oversight.

A prime example of this phenomenon at work was presented in the material on Congressman Cornelius Gallagher in chapter 4. It is always difficult to say exactly what stimulates a person to action. For Congressman Gallagher, constituent complaints constituted one stimulus to seek authority to form the Special Subcommittee on the Invasion of Privacy. But once Gallagher emerged as a powerful and public defender of privacy, telephone calls and mail flooded into his office both from within his district and from elsewhere providing him with new data and case studies of alleged abuses of privacy. Once the SSIP was formed, Gallagher had a reservoir of material to push. Direct action emerged from an interest partly stimulated and reinforced by casework. For Gallagher, casework led to information which led to investigations and legislation.[30]

Several indirect results for oversight emerged from casework; more direct results were also found. Primarily, direct action took the form of making floor speeches, of conducting or seeking investigations, and introducing bills for legislation. Exhaustive data on how frequently casework leads to investigations or legislation is scarce. The following very fragmentary data gathered as part of the interviews for the case studies in chapters 2 through 5 is at least suggestive. Forty-one interviewees were asked, "How frequently does casework lead to an investigation or to the introduction of legislation?" Their responses follow:

Never	0	Frequently	8
Seldom	13	Usually or normally	1
From time to time	4	No answer	7

At least as perceived by these participants, casework did at times lead to direct oversight activity. The easiest public response to a constituent's problem is to take the floor of the House or Senate and protest against alleged bureaucratic bungling. Such behavior is not unknown in the Congress. It is more difficult to launch an investigation of the general problems symbolized in the specific constituent complaint. The ability to mount such an investigation is conditioned by factors other than one's interest. One's committee assignments, status on these committees, access to key persons and relevant committees, and a series of related factors previously discussed influence one's ability to strike out in an investigation. Partly because of these difficulties, "it is usually an accident—or a particularly flagrant abuse—that leads to a full-scale investigation and the necessary remedial legislation."[31]

One example of how these sequences work was found in the hearings held by the Senate Constitutional Rights Subcommittee in June 1965, entitled *Psychological Testing and Constitutional Rights*. Federal employees, recognizing the subcommittee as a vocal defender of their rights, deluged it with examples of the alleged abuses of these rights: "The subcommittee has received and investigated numerous complaints that Federal employees are being subjected to mind-probing sessions with Government psychiatrists and psychologists under threat of undergoing disciplinary action or losing their jobs."[32]

A similar situation, but clearer because of its origins in a single case, developed when a constituent of Representative Durward Hall's (R.–Missouri) complained that his mail was being seized by postal officials and being turned over to the Internal Revenue Service. On the basis of this information, Senator Edward V. Long (D.–Missouri), chairman of the

Senate Subcommittee on Administrative Practice and Procedure, launched an investigation and held a hearing to expose the practice and condemn it.[33]

Constituent complaints only infrequently result in the drafting or introduction of legislation. Yet most congressmen interviewed did cite a few examples of such behavior. Usually ignored in the newspaper headlines, these actions nonetheless could be of considerable consequence to large groups of individuals.

Each congressman interviewed was asked whether any of his casework led him to introduce a bill in the 89th or 90th Congress to correct a policy problem. The examples below illustrate the results of the inquiry. The list of topics indicates the range of these activities:

The effect of blindness on benefits provided for in Title 2 of the Social Security Act (Olsen, Montana)

To amend the Universal Military Training and Service Act to exempt certain individuals from induction (Broyhill, North Carolina)

Compensation for employees of the United States for performing inspection and quarantine services on Sundays and holidays (Matsunaga, Hawaii)

Regulating the conditions under which dogs and cats are used for purposes of experimentation (Matsunaga, Hawaii)

To amend the Federal Credit Union Act (Matsunaga, Hawaii)

To exclude from income certain reimbursed moving expenses (Matsunaga, Hawaii)

To provide income tax deductions for contributions to conservation organizations (Tunney, California)

To increase health benefits for dependents of the Uniform Services (Tunney, California)

To prohibit political influence in appointments, etc. in the postal field service (Gross, Iowa)

To establish a small tax division within the Tax Court of the United States (Ellsworth, Kansas)

To enable leasehold farmers in Hawaii to obtain farm improvement loans (Matsunaga, Hawaii)

Casework under rare circumstances can lead to legislation being introduced on controversial public questions. An example involved the effort of Congressman Jackson Betts (R.–Ohio) to reduce the number of compulsory questions for the United States Census in 1970. Responding to a complaint from an elderly couple in his district, Congressman Betts came later to introduce such legislation and to gain major support for it. Writing in the *New York Times*, Nan Robertson explained the success of the crusade: "It has combined good timing, and constant harping on a small and easily graspable theme."[34] Thus, she illustrated also how the complexity of the subject matter relates to oversight.

If casework did not frequently induce the Congress to address the trauma-inducing issues of the day, it did move the Congress toward action on many problems of concern to more than a few isolated individuals. The consequences of casework for oversight activity were clear: Congressional activity was substantial but not overwhelming.

The eruption of a case into a major public issue was often an index of the fact that informal consultation and negotiation had broken down and that the congressmen felt that the issue was important enough to press formally. A subcommittee staff director reported: "I take complaints of bureaucrats to the top levels of the executive departments to talk about the problems involved. I try and meet informally first . . . and then proceed beyond that only if necessary. It isn't necessary very often." Another committee staff member suggested that "informally there is much contact back and forth between the committees' staff and the executive. This contact does not appear in the record of formal investigations."

Evidence is scarce about the latent functions performed by casework; it is almost nonexistent about the actual impact of congressional casework inquiries on administrative behavior. The lore on the subject takes two directions: (1) that of a quaking bureaucracy, fearful of not accommodating any congressional whim; (2) that of a bureaucracy angry at, and unreceptive to, congressional interference and meddling. The incidental evidence gathered along the route of this research does not encourage any firm resolution of this issue, but it does contribute some insight into the relationships between casework and executive behavior.

First, it is clear that congressional involvement does result in increasing the likelihood of bureaucratic attention to the constituent's case. Testifying before a House Appropriations Subcommittee in 1965, Deputy Postmaster General Fred Belen asserted:

> *I know that when I first became Assistant Postmaster General for Operations, I received about as many congressional letters as any official in Washington. On an average of 300 congressional letters were received each day. Early each morning I read every congressional letter. Almost all these letters were individual complaints. Here we were dealing with a squeaky-wheel theory. You can't take a complaint even though it may involve a minor grievance in a post office and write a Congressman back and say, "Well, it just isn't so." The individual knows what happened and in order to make a proper response, it had to be investigated. This was quite a workload, in itself. We did give attention to it.*[35]

Executive departments are so immersed in these transactions that John Macy, chairman of the Civil Service Commission, could refer to them as the executive's "retail business."

Executive attention sometimes varies with the form of the request. J. Edward Day, former postmaster general, suggested that a congressional letter will often draw simply a routine response. Only if the member of Congress showed real interest, meaning a telephone call or a personal visit, Day asserted, did the request get additional attention.[36] All of this occurs despite a fairly widespread distaste for congressional interference. Most are not as vehement as one legislative liaison man: "This job would be the greatest ever if it were not for this constituent crap. I get buckets of it and have to handle it."

Beyond drawing executive attention to an area, casework sometimes did bring forth a problem area of which top-ranking officials were unaware or to which they had been unresponsive previously. In 1965, cotton farmers in California had written to the Department of Agriculture about technical problems raised for them under new omnibus farm legislation. Receiving insufficient satisfaction from the department, farm groups then successfully sought congressional intervention. The department wrote to California congressmen assuring them that a top-level Agriculture Department representative would meet with the farmers. In the words of the letter to a California congressman: "These conferences disclosed the need for prompt issuance of a clarification of the national procedures for determining farm conserving bases." The Department of Agriculture clearly became more sensitive to the policy problems represented by this case than it was prior to congressional involvement.[37]

Rarer than drawing attention to an area or stimulating an awareness of a defective policy was the situation where executive departments and agencies actually revised or altered their decisions or policies as a result of congressional casework. Such cases rarely resulted in major upheavals on issues that threatened the foundations of the political system, but they did affect substantial numbers of people on issues that were vital to *them*. Several examples illustrate the range of congressional success: Congressman Robert Corbett (R.—Pennsylvania) succeeded in gaining a refund from the Internal Revenue Service for a citizen who was charged "improperly" for an Internal Revenue mistake;[38] Senator Sam Ervin pressured the Federal Aviation Administration in a Montana office to reverse a warning to employees about the consequences of filing grievances;[39] in response to a complaint from Senator Ervin, the Army canceled an order telling active-duty personnel that they could not display political bumper stickers on their cars.[40]

No one should assume that congressional requests were routinely met; at times, even the most vigorous protests were to no avail. Congressman James Morrison reported a 1943 experience in which he complained to the OPA about prices of Louisiana potatoes:

> *The potato farmers of Louisiana are raising hell and I do not blame them. . . . I have written letters until I am blue in the face. I have talked this over with officials until I am sick at my stomach. I have received letters of complaint from people in my district until I never want to see another letter with the name potato in it. And yet I can do nothing. I can get nothing.*[41]

Perhaps the most substantial impacts of casework on executive behavior have occurred when a case led to an inquiry which then created a climate of concern which in turn affected subsequent decisions. The data in chapter 4 dealing with invasion of privacy provided outstanding examples of this phenomenon.

It is not too difficult to demonstrate the relevance of casework for oversight. The pages above have spelled out more precisely what some of that relevance might be. Yet it makes little sense to argue that casework is a major element in effective oversight. Preventing this is the principal focus of much casework: namely, an effort to provide an answer to a single complaint without concern for an overall pattern that this complaint might represent.

The top executive official who derided the casework efforts of one committee ("They are preoccupied with trivia") is focusing on casework only from the perspective of its limits. The judgment arising from my own research is closer to that of Dale Vinyard who, after studying the efforts of the Senate and the House committees on small business, concluded:

> *The total policy impact of such activities probably is not great. Sometimes it may personalize policy avoiding the rigidities of general rules and regulations. There are instances where substantial grievances are uncovered and corrective action taken. Also there are many cases where the efforts are merely pro forma and do not result in any change. But in such instances, individuals or groups at least have the hearing which may provide a measure of satisfaction to them.*[42]

Reports Required by Legislation

In 1957, J. Malcolm Smith and Cornelius P. Cotter suggested that an analysis of reports required of the executive departments and agencies by the Congress would be useful. [43] As a first step toward such an effort they presented data on reports required in defense and emergency statutes since early in the 1930s. Congress continues to require these reports in large numbers. The Joint Committee on the Organization of the Congress reported that 639 annual reports were required in 1966.[44]

As part of the research for chapters 2 through 5, an effort was made to gain some insight into why such reporting procedures were used, how extensively they were used, and how participants in the legislative process viewed these uses. Only some thirty interviewees commented on the reporting procedure, so no firm findings emerge. Rather, these findings are offered in the "Gellhorn spirit" that something may be better than nothing.

Interviewees asserted that formal reporting procedures were used in two types of circumstances: (1) in a subject area in which congressmen felt that an unusual amount of supervision was required; (2) to get information where informal consultation processes had broken down. Congressmen implicitly assumed, in each situation, that required reports were an effective means toward closer legislative oversight of the bureaucracy. As we will see shortly, there is some reason to doubt that this is the case.

When reports were required, it was presumed that they would provide information useful to the Congress, that they would facilitate two-way executive-legislative communication, and that the need to prepare the reports would stimulate executive departments toward more self-evaluation and toward more sensitivity to the presence and requirements of the Congress. Some data will be provided below for the first two presumptions. The third, perhaps the most important of all, remains to be studied elsewhere. On the last point, a House Judiciary Committee staff member stated the prevailing sense among staff persons when he asserted: "These reports *should* stimulate executive attention to Congress, but I don't know if they really do."

Congress requires the executive departments to report extensively. As Table 6 indicates, congressional requirements for formal reports cut across a wide variety of departments, agencies, and programs within them. Also indicated is that periodic efforts to prune the number of reports, as in 1965, seemed to be only temporarily successful. The number required, when cut, quickly rises again. Perhaps as in the reduction in the number of standing committees, which in turn led to the proliferation of subcommittees, durability attests to the performance of a function at least perceived as being useful by participants in the legislative process. A partial explanation for this record of durability is, of course, that some of these reports were perceived as useful. But what about all the rest of the reports? Some insight into the utility of such reports for oversight purposes can be derived from how these reports were used.

One index of utility is usage; usage assumes access. No congressman or staff assistant reported that his office or committee had a systematic procedure for preserving and

TABLE 6: Reports to Be Made by the Executive
Departments to the Congress

Department	1963	1966	1969
State	57	50	54
Treasury	18	19	16
Defense	75	71	90
Justice	20	22	22
Post Office	7	6	9
Interior	63	80	93
Agriculture	9	9	11
Commerce	30	41	27
Labor	15	13	12
Health, Education, and Welfare	19	35	63
Transportation	—	—	35
Housing and Urban Development	—	10	28

Source: Data compiled from U.S. Congress, House of Representatives, 88th Congress, 1st sess., Doc. 23, "Reports to be Made to Congress," January 1963; 89th Congress, 2d sess., H. Doc. 343, "Reports to be Made to Congress," January 1966; 91st Congress, 1st sess., H. Doc. 31, "Reports to be Made to Congress," January 1969. These figures are only indicative of the pattern because some of the reports are required more than once yearly, others are required only on request, some are prepared elsewhere and submitted by the department named, and some are prepared in the department named but formally submitted by another source. Some of the data above were compiled by Barbara Laughlin Mann.

filing executive reports as received. Furthermore, no one reported any strong sense of deprivation because such files were not maintained. There was a similar reaction to inquiries as to whether these reports were read. Most were not, but a few members did say that they glanced at some reports. In a classic statement of an information overload thesis, one member asserted: "We have to keep the wastebaskets full to survive." Committee staff members reported that some of these reports merited a careful glance before disposal. Like the members of the Congress, staff members related a strong correlation between their own prior concern with the subject matter and the probability that they would read a report carefully.

On the basis of this limited sampling, it seemed that these reports were of little use to all members or to all of the staff. The flavor of their comments was captured in a paper prepared in 1962 by former congressman Byron L. Johnson: "The right of Congress to require *reporting* by the Executive is absolutely clear. Yet over the years, as the recipient of many such reports, I frequently found them of limited value."[45] Given the extensive division of labor in the Congress, this "finding" should startle no one.

Of more interest is that a similar, if not as emphatic, conclusion emerged from interviews with persons about their fields of specialization. Only two interviewees felt that these reports were very useful, and one of these based his conclusion not so much on actual experience but on a more general assumption about human behavior. "Men are lazy and self-willed, so this type of procedure stimulates them to re-examine, to reinvigorate themselves, and to be concerned with Congress."

About a third of the interviewees made statements echoing a single theme: "I don't put much stock in them." Others asserted that only a few reports were useful; they offered no explanation as to why most reports were used so infrequently. More members of the Congress suggested that short-term authorizations could achieve the same ends more effectively than spoke affirmatively about the utility of required reports.

Some interviewees thought the process of preparing required reports did in fact sensitize the executive; an equal number thought otherwise. The largest group simply speculated that requiring reports *should* sensitize the executive, but they were not confident that this goal was accomplished.

A hypothesis that may help explain why some reports were asked for relates to their latent function. Required reports have as their manifest function the promotion of legislative oversight; these reports may be more important because of a latent function performed—assertion of jurisdiction for a congressional committee or subcommittee. As a highly regarded staff director concluded: "Where committee jurisdiction is unclear, each committee will attempt to gain prescriptive jurisdiction through requiring reports by an executive department to it. Oversight activity on the surface is really being used as a tool in committee rivalry."

Overall, despite their numbers, required reports seemed with a few exceptions to make a rather modest contribution to oversight. They seemed more useful to those individuals waiting for them than to those who received them more routinely. Perhaps their greatest impact was on those who prepared them, rather than those who received them. Without further data, this judgment can only be called informed speculation.[46]

From a psychological viewpoint, perhaps the most fascinating question is why those who selected this device did so. Other than the few fragmentary insights provided above, information remains difficult to discover. Those in this small sample who used this device seldom articulated an explanation of their choice; those who did not use the reports were tolerant of the efforts of those who did, but asserted that they really could not explain why some did choose this method. Although some felt that requiring reports enhanced the congressional capability for oversight, evidence in support of these intuitions is slight.

Ultimately an explanation may rest on the fact that so few techniques that give promise of effectiveness are as easily applied. The symbolic value of an act which "seems to accomplish something concrete" and can be easily applied should not be underrated. Perhaps this is why the recommendations of the Joint Committee on the Organization of Congress for "review [of] all reports required by existing laws to determine if they fill a useful function"[47] is likely only to result in very modest changes in usage.

The analysis in this chapter of legislative hearings, casework, and reports required by the Congress suggests that much oversight activity has taken place during legislative activities not labeled oversight or commonly associated with it. The dimensions of legislative oversight activity are broader than is often acknowledged.[48] Awareness of the latent performance of oversight is required for a full comprehension of its dimensions. Adding latent to manifest oversight leaves unaltered the intermittent and noncomprehensive character of the performance of the function.

Chapter 7 Legislative Oversight in the Present and in the Future

Knowledge about legislative oversight of bureaucracy is growing cumulatively. Yet what is not known is still substantial. Both of these generalizations gain support as the findings herein are added to those from other research. These conclusions fit into three categories: (1) those concerning the motivations and behavior of congressmen in the area of oversight; (2) those relating structural factors in the Congress to oversight; (3) those demonstrating the impact of congressional efforts.[1]

The Congressmen and Oversight

There is consensus in the Congress that comprehensive and systematic oversight *ought* to be conducted.[2] Many interviewees expressed a sense of regret that they were not doing more. The attention to oversight in the Legislative Reorganization Act of 1970 and in the Congressional Budget and Impoundment Control Act of 1974 provided additional evidence of a general concern by congressmen for improving its performance.

Despite their evident sincerity in acknowledging a general obligation to oversee, few members felt any strong stimulus to fulfill this obligation regularly. The gap between expectations and behavior was large. The general feeling that oversight is something that one should do does not help much to explain what is actually done.[3] Apparently other factors are decisive in shaping the members' decisions whether or not to oversee.

Many members were occasionally involved in oversight activity; few really did very much about it. Most members assigned a relatively low priority to oversight and hence spent little time on it. Kenneth Kofmehl similarly found that congressional committees give oversight a priority second to lawmaking and that committee staff persons spend a small percentage of their time on it.[4]

An especially low priority was given to oversight by those members who disliked their committee assignments. Two reasons most frequently offered for disliking committee assignments were low perceived political salience for the member and a lack of interest in the subject matter within the committee's jurisdiction. The experience reported in chapters 2 and 3 provides strong supportive evidence. John Bibby's study of the Senate Banking and Currency Committee points in the same direction.[5]

If a member gives a low priority to oversight, those items assigned a higher priority will capture his time. When the priorities set do not implicitly limit the possibility of attention to oversight, what is done is affected by member confidence in agency personnel,[6] previous treatment by executive agencies, which political party controls the Congress and the presidency,[7] and the other opportunity factors. Congressmen with high opportunity factors try to oversee most frequently in the presence of some of the conversion factors.

The cases studied in the preceding chapters provide ample evidence in support of Scher's thesis that members calculate personal gains and losses before they undertake oversight activity. In this gain-loss calculus, oversight is frequently seen as less central than legislating and serving one's district more directly.[8]

There is no necessary incompatibility between legislating, serving one's constituents effectively, and overseeing the bureaucracy. But since the legislator's primary focus is typically elsewhere than on oversight, the general obligation to oversee will tend to be fulfilled mainly as other purposes are being served. Legislators are most concerned with issues that they perceive as highly relevant to their political survival.[9]

The Structure of the Congress and Oversight

Almost all legislative oversight is conducted by the standing committees and subcommittees of the Congress. A modest fraction comes from individual members as they process casework. Even in such situations, the member often takes his problem to the relevant committee.

Committee oversight efforts are infrequently coordinated and at times are even undertaken for conflicting purposes. The Special Subcommittee on the Invasion of Privacy of the House Government Operations Committee and the Constitutional Rights Subcommittee of the Senate Judiciary Committee both studied the use of personality testing in federal hiring, but each "went its own way." On civil rights questions, the House and the Senate Judiciary Committees heard different drummers. The House Post Office and Civil Service Committee and its counterpart in the Senate also failed to coordinate their oversight activity.

Emmette S. Redford identifies an additional consequence of uncoordinated oversight efforts:

> *A dissentient group may shop from one counter to another in Congress in search for a channel through which it can market its desire for influence upon administration. . . . The informal contacts and the lack of a tradition against action in detail accentuate the atomization of control. The result is that from a multitude of directions the pieces of Congress pick at the administration at many little points.*[10]

These differences are indicative of the wide variety of committee behavior on oversight.[11] Chapters 2 through 5 provided examples of a committee that was very active, one that was moderately so, and one that was somnolent.

In explaining differences in committee behavior, students of oversight commonly find links between the structure of power within a committee and the conduct of oversight. The importance of committee and subcommittee chairmen is a central finding. One interview with a veteran member of the House captured the situation. After some polite fencing as he answered questions that he regarded as trivial, he offered incisive answers as the questions swung toward the relevance of the committee chairman for oversight. The member's delight was scarcely concealed as he began his answer with "Now you're on to something *really* important!" The evidence herein confirms the following conclusion by J. Leiper Freeman: "The substantive committee leaders tend to constitute the most constant congressional influentials in subsystem policy-making. They are frequently able to exercise a major degree of censorship over the final legislative product; especially is this true of the veteran members of the committee in-group."[12]

The best boost for an active oversight effort is a committee chairman who puts a high premium on oversight and has the skill and resources to do something about it. The next best option is a permissive committee chairman who yields enough autonomy to his subcommittee heads that they can function effectively if they desire to do so.

Chairman Celler of the Judiciary Committee sought to frustrate formal oversight efforts in civil rights during the 89th and 90th Congresses. He was mainly successful. If he had desired more oversight, he could have had it. Chairman Dawson of the Government Operations Committee was no passionate devotee of oversight. His willingness to grant some measure of subcommittee autonomy made it possible for the

SSIP to function. The energy and initiative of Subcommittee Chairman Gallagher provided the mainspring of SSIP activity. Perhaps the SSIP conducted more oversight than Dawson might have wanted.

The Post Office and Civil Service Committee reorganized itself in the 89th Congress to escape the inactivity of the chairman and to promote subcommittee autonomy. The experience was clearly a mixed one. Some of the new subcommittees, such as Manpower Utilization, were vigorous in oversight efforts; most subcommittees were not as active. Prior to the reorganization, Chairman Murray's unwillingness to act had been used as a basic excuse. After the "revolution," other explanations needed to be found.

Few underestimate the importance of committee chairmen for oversight. Many overestimate the importance of the staff. A standard shibboleth about the Congress correlates increasing the size of the staff with improving congressional performance. Whatever commentators may assert, the congressmen and the staff people interviewed felt that beyond a minimum level, more staff did not necessarily mean more or better work.[13] The consensus seemed to be that the major limits came more from the member's priorities and hence his allocation of his time than from any shortage of staff.

The Impact of Congressional Efforts

Specific oversight efforts such as that of the SSIP on the data bank issue can have a substantial impact.[14] Overall, congressional influence tends to be more scattered and slight. Oversight efforts seen to alert executive agencies to problems and to stimulate reexamination more than to provide comprehensive and systematic direction and control. In most situations, the basic explanation for modest amounts of oversight is found in the way that congressmen and their staffs choose to spend their time and energy. Motivation is the key factor, not competence. In this sense, structure and priority-setting are mutually reinforcing. The Congress is not organized to maximize its impact, and individual members frequently feel that they have other things to do which are more important than oversight.

There is widespread agreement that legislative oversight is neither comprehensive nor systematic. Ralph K. Huitt summarizes the research: "Not much 'oversight' of administration in a systematic and continuous enough manner to make it mean very much, is practiced. The appropriations committees probably do more than the legislative committees . . . and the House Appropriations Committee does more than the Senate committee."[15]

The data in the present research surely support this conclusion. It is also true that more oversight occurs than is commonly acknowledged. Conventional analysis has paid insufficient attention to oversight other than formal investigations. Chapter 6 shows that the extent of latent oversight performed by the Congress needs to be seriously assessed. Casework, legislative hearings, and informal member and staff contacts with bureaucrats do not appear in many tally sheets as oversight, but they certainly ought to.[16]

Reform Proposals

Do these findings help in assessing proposals for changes in congressional conduct of oversight? They surely do.

Almost all proposals for reforming the conduct of legislative oversight embody ideas for structural reforms. The reason for this emphasis is easy to glean. Structure is a visible and significant element in legislative decision-making. Besides, tinkering with legislative structure is easier than trying to alter member priorities. The number of proposals for structural reform has been immense. Some examples illustrate the variety offered.

JCOC Proposal of 1966

First, consider the proposals made by the Joint Committee on the Organization of Congress (JCOC) in 1966. The members of the JCOC, supported by an able staff, found it difficult intellectually and pragmatically to cope adequately with the problems of oversight. One staff member involved in thinking about oversight lamented the quality of ideas presented for committee consideration. He reported:

> *There is a general paucity of ideas in this area [oversight]. It wasn't that there were a series of ideas and a variety were rejected on various counts. Basically, the only two suggestions considered were a separate oversight committee, which was rejected, and the idea of a review specialist for each standing committee, which was accepted.*

A staff member on another committee scoffed at the JCOC proposal for a review specialist, pointing out that the new staff member, even if titled a review specialist, would inevitably be drawn toward the committee's work rather than redirecting committee efforts. Nearly all interviewees questioned the utility of the proposal.

The JCOC seemed to assume that staff size and information available were central factors in determining legislative behavior on oversight. The analysis in this study points in other directions.

Oversight Subcommittees

Some congressmen have long urged each standing committee to create an oversight subcommittee. As noted above, such a proposal was rejected by the JCOC. But fashions change. Without clear evidence of whether the few existing oversight subcommittees had been effective, the House of Representatives voted in 1974 to require each standing committee, except for Appropriations and Budget, either to establish an oversight subcommittee or to order each of its subcommittees to conduct oversight.[17] Whether this step indicates altered member priorities or merely provides the appearance of progress will be seen as experience accumulates.

Legislative Reorganization Act of 1946

The Legislative Reorganization Act of 1946 gave the Congress a strong oversight mandate. Davidson, Kovenock, and O'Leary, some twenty years later, commented on the experience with this broad grant of authority: "With regard to the federal bureaucracy, Congress ought to provide the 'continuous watchfulness' specified by the Legislative Reorganization Act of 1946. Unfortunately, too few committees have fulfilled this responsibility; the reasons for this failure would themselves comprise a lengthy study."[18]

In 1965, at hearings held by the Joint Committee on the Organization of Congress, Davidson had presented a similar thought: "I would not want to make a blanket statement but I think it is true. Many of the legislative committees have, as you suggest, not been as careful as they might have been in following the mandate of the 1946 act, which was to exercise continuous watchfulness over the agencies under their jurisdiction. I don't know why this is."[19]

Twenty years of experience suggest that the absence of authority to oversee seldom explains why the Congress does not oversee more comprehensively or systematically.

The case studies herein show that no single answer fully explains why committees do not conduct more oversight. At least four categories of reasons help to move an analysis forward.

1. The members on some committees and subcommittees exhibit modest concern for the committee's work. On these committees, comprehensive oversight is unlikely to get much attention. The experience of the House Post Office and Civil Service Committee in 1965–1967 provides a sterling example.

2. On some committees, members are active and interested but perform little formal oversight because legislation captures their primary attention. In such contexts, one should expect to find significant latent oversight. The record of the House Judiciary Committee provides an instructive example.

3. On some committees, the members in charge have determined that more oversight will not serve their partisan and policy purposes. In these situations, the duty to oversee is normally subordinated. The desire to oversee is successfully repressed.

4. On relatively few subcommittees, a lack of continuing authority and adequate resources is an important limit. The full committee chairman usually can allocate the necessary resources and authority, if he chooses to do so. The experience of the Special Subcommittee on the Invasion of Privacy is illustrative.

The Legislative Reorganization Act of 1970

In 1970 Congress passed another reform bill, the Legislative Reorganization Act of 1970.[20] One section of the act requires each standing committee of the House and Senate to "review and study, on a continuing basis, the application, administration, and execution of those laws, or parts of laws, the subject of which is within the jurisdiction of that committee." This grant of authority restates the essence of the 1946 Reorganization Act, which provides a general obligation to oversee. Experience suggests that the impact of this injunction will be minimal.

A second provision requires each standing committee, with a few stated exceptions, to submit a biennial report of its oversight activities. A reporting requirement does not by itself force committee action, but having to account for one's behavior does seem to provide a modest incentive to pay more heed to oversight. Still, few would regard this reporting clause as a major step toward altering legislative behavior.

A section calling for annual appropriations wherever possible is more meaningful. The most extensive, and perhaps the most effective oversight done in the House and the Senate comes in the yearly reviews of the appropriations committees.

Roger Davidson notes:

> *I think the implication of our statement was that the appropriations process itself was an important, perhaps the most important, aspect of oversight precisely because it is addressed to specific problems where the committee has to say "up" or "down" on specific sums of money. I think the implication of our remarks was that it is probably the most effective single instrument of oversight which the Congress has.* [21]

Because they are faced with documents making concrete proposals, these committees may pay more regular attention to specific problems than do the authorizing committees. Routines are set partly in response to concrete pressures imposed by the tyranny of schedules.

The provision of the 1970 Act substituting the term "review" for "oversight" requires no comment.

Beyond these specific changes, the provisions of the Legislative Reorganization Act which tended to distribute power more widely within standing committees should indirectly increase the opportunity for oversight.

Oversight Calendar

Writing in 1966, Cornelius Cotter proposed some changes designed to improve legislative oversight. Some of these, such as the recommendation for a question period, have been the staple of discussions elsewhere in the literature. One distinctive proposal relating to oversight was that "the House and the Senate should establish oversight calendars, giving precedence at least two days in each month, to committee reports pertaining to oversight of administration." [22]

The analysis in the present study suggests that the proposal for an oversight calendar would probably accomplish little. Most effective oversight is done at the committee level, not on the floor of either house. If the members are as busy as they say they are, they are unlikely, simply because these items will appear on a calendar, to prepare for the kind of discussion that would be necessary for effective oversight. The consequences of such a proposal are surely opaque.

These proposals, like others for structural change, seem mainly a response to symptoms rather than to causes. The complexity of oversight problems and the modest understanding of them at present may mean that only symptomatic treatment is possible. Complex problems are always difficult to address at their core.

Oversight in the Legislative Process

Bureaucratic Responsibility

If the reforms discussed seem inadequate for what they are designed to achieve, is legislative oversight of the bureaucracy likely to continue in its widely varied and fitful state? This is the broader question of what does where we have been tell us about where we are going.

Holding bureaucracy accountable in a modern, complex, industrial society presents immense problems. The need itself guarantees no solution. Fortunately, achieving bureaucratic responsibility does not rest solely on congressional efforts.[23]

Many factors contribute to the responsible behavior of federal employees, not the least of which is that most of them accept the values of a society which calls upon them to act responsibly. In addition, many are trained professionally to act with skill, competence, and a measure of dispassion.

Beyond the realm of ingrained values and training, there are formal sanctions and incentives available to promote conduct in conformity with the demands of the political realms of American society. Rules are set up to punish errant bureaucrats. Incentives such as promotion, transfers, and salary increases help to hold bureaucrats accountable. Financial controls both within the bureaucracy and from the Congress and such agencies as the General Accounting Office not only root out deviant behavior but also cause bureaucrats to think before they act. What Carl Friedrich calls the law of anticipated reaction seems to be an important means of holding bureaucrats responsible; if bureaucrats anticipate that their actions will be inspected by other units of the bureaucracy, by the Congress, and perhaps by the courts, they are more likely to act with a sense of responsibility.[24]

So restraints on the bureaucracy are not simply a function of external checks imposed by the Congress and the courts. They are also based on elements within the bureaucracy itself.

The Limits of Induction

What, then, can we say about the contribution of legislative oversight? A caution is worth restating. In political analysis as in literature, the slice-of-life approach, viewing human behavior over a short period of time, has its problems. Today's reality and insight may not capture the full picture. What is central to explaining what happens today may be peripheral tomorrow.

Since the research and analysis for these chapters was completed, direction and control of the postal service has passed to an independent government agency, the U.S. Postal Service; the flood of civil rights legislation has receded to a trickle; and the SSIP has been abolished by a new committee chairman. Still, these case studies provide an explanation of relationships as they were in a given period of time, suggest some insights into how they might operate more generally, and illustrate the utility of particular types of analysis.

The dangers of generalizing about legislative oversight from limited data are not only those resulting from the limited time period involved.[25] Legislative oversight may operate differently in committees not studied. Until enough case studies are done to provide a firmer basis for generalization, there always remains some peril in using the inductive method.

The Quantity of Oversight

Most writers about legislative oversight have not been very kind to the Congress. Most conclude that legislative oversight has been sporadic, atomized, erratic, trivial, ineffective, or some combination of these. Perhaps the analysis of Leonard D. White, in his presidential address prepared for the American Political Science Association in 1945, comes close to being typical. White charges that the Congress tinkers with "detail not over essentials." He asserts that legislative oversight is often "negative and repressive rather than positive and constructive." There is "no rational plan" to what the Congress does in the oversight area; rather, what oversight exists "is an accumulation of particulars."[26]

Discussions of what oversight the Congress has performed usually end up focusing on what the Congress has not done. The eye of the critic tends to be on the need for systematic, overall assessment of each program that the Congress has established and might monitor. If systematic and comprehensive inquiry is the standard, then the Congress clearly has not met the mark.

Many analysts have portrayed the demise of the Congress in legislating. Some have accompanied this dirge with comments about the relatively greater capacity of the Congress for oversight only to conclude that the Congress oversees badly. From this line of analysis, the decline-of-Congress thesis flows easily.

Whether they label the amount of oversight that the Congress is doing as "high" or "low," many observers agree that the amount of legislative oversight has increased since World War II.[27] Supporting evidence is seen in the data presented in table 7 concerning trends in spending in con-

TABLE 7: Expenditures by Select, Special, and Standing Congressional Committees for Investigations

	House of Representatives	Senate
85th Congress		
1957–1958	$4,870,996	$5,777,335
86th Congress		
1959–1960	4,931,886	6,961,169
87th Congress		
1961–1962	5,756,984	7,165,387
88th Congress		
1963–1964	7,484,743	7,716,821
89th Congress		
1965–1966	8,105,358	9,689,347
90th Congress		
1967–1968	10,825,855	11,168,988

Source: These data were compiled by Lynette P. Perkins from committee totals in the Congressional Quarterly Almanac *and in the* Congressional Quarterly Weekly Report *for the relevant years. Both are published in Washington, D.C., by* Congressional Quarterly Service, Inc.

gressional investigations. Table 7 shows that the Congress is increasingly spending more money for investigations. The figures, however, tell us little about the scope or quality of congressional efforts or about their impact. These data can be easily interpreted to show more than they actually do. In addition, one needs to reflect over whether formal investigations are a good index of oversight activity.

If there are difficulties in determining the exact amount of oversight performed, there are even more in assessing the quality of oversight, since judgments about quality are so intertwined with value perspectives. Is a study which condemns the Bureau of the Budget for wanting to set up a national data bank but which does not deal with questions of efficiency and economy a "good study" or not? The answer depends on the values that one brings to the analysis. If a national data bank is viewed as a strong threat to personal privacy and if one places a high value on such privacy, then the Special Subcommittee on the Invasion of Privacy did an excellent job. If one is more concerned with saving governmental money, with developing more efficient records, and with having data available for research by scholars, then the SSIP efforts might be viewed as one-sided and perhaps harmful. Judgment and perspective are too closely related to be considered separately for very long.

If one is concerned primarily with working conditions for postal employees, then one might applaud the House Post Office and Civil Service Committee for attacking the practice of using stopwatches to monitor the work of postal employees. If a more important concern is efficiency in the Post Office, then one might view the use of stopwatches as an appropriate, even if psychologically disturbing, technique.

Very few investigations by any congressional committee are universally acclaimed. The work of the so-called Truman Committee during World War II in investigating aspects of the war effort has usually been so regarded.[28] Opinion divides more readily concerning the usual oversight efforts undertaken by most committees and subcommittees.

There is both qualitative and quantitative variation in the oversight efforts of committees. It thus becomes very difficult to talk about the efforts at oversight by the Congress as a whole. Compounding this problem is that even within the same committee, some subcommittees are active, alert, and productive in oversight, while others are either inert or inactive by almost any standard.

Barriers to Perfect Performance
Congressional oversight activity cannot fulfill the requirements of the reorganization acts of 1946 and 1970 because these statutes set excessive expectations. Besides, many factors in the legislative process work against any

drastic increase in oversight activity. The structure of the Congress, for example, imposes barriers. As long as the Congress is bicameral and the committees in each house are unwilling to coordinate with their counterparts in the other house, and as long as there are numerous standing committees and subcommittees in both houses with relative freedom to go their own way in investigating problems, the conduct of oversight will be difficult to alter substantially. These factors, deeply rooted within the legislative process, inhibit any sharp increase in the quantity and quality of oversight performed.

The constituency orientation of the legislators reinforces this picture. Most congressmen act primarily to serve their constituents so as to promote the member's political survival. As long as what gets a congressman reelected is something other than systematic oversight, and that is likely to be the case in the indefinite future, the typical congressman will not drastically alter his priorities to pursue a lesser grail.

Some Possible Trends

If the Congress cannot perfect its performance of the oversight function, in what directions might it move? The analysis of Samuel P. Huntington provides an organizing focus.[29] Huntington, in a brilliant and provocative (if flawed) essay, traces the evolution of congressional functions and then projects three possible paths for the future of the Congress.

One alternative is that congressmen would live with the frustrations that they face and continue "on the verge of stalemate and breakdown." A second possibility that Huntington outlines is a fundamental restructuring of power relationships in the Congress. Such a revolution would render obsolete most analyses of existing operations. A third alternative is for the Congress consciously to redefine its functions: to recognize that oversight has become its primary function, that legislation has become a more marginal activity, and then to behave accordingly.

Huntington concluded that it is entirely possible that "neither adaptation nor reform is necessary."[30] As long as the Congress acts astutely and does not stymie the operations of the political system, the present may indeed predict the future.

Huntington is not very sanguine about fundamentally restructuring power relationships within the Congress. He cites two types of proposals for the basic reform of Congress, those put forth by "democratisers" and those suggested by "party reformers," neither of which "is likely, if enacted, to achieve the results which its principal proponents desire."[31]

The third possibility Huntington calls "adaptation and reform." He sees this process as more probable politically even though it would involve great strains on the psyches of congressmen. In essence, the Congress would simply recognize what has been happening to it: It has lost its legislative function and needs to intensify attention to those aspects of the legislative process that it is most competent to handle, namely, casework and oversight. Huntington cites previous examples of an institution redirecting itself in response to changed circumstances in the society. He asks whether the Congress might not do the same thing.

> *Explicit acceptance of the idea that legislation was not its primary function would, in large part, simply be recognition of the direction which change has already been taking. It would legitimize and expand the functions of constituent service and administrative oversight which, in practice, already constitute the principal work of most congressmen.*[32]

The impressive sweep of Huntington's analysis masks several problems. The first is his comparative assessment of the congressional capacity to legislate and to oversee. Huntington argues that the Congress can oversee more effectively than it can legislate because of its decentralized nature.

This conclusion ignores the powerful factors in the legislative process inhibiting congressional efforts at oversight. Thus, one needs to be cautious. But secondly, the associations between legislation and the Congress as a whole, and between oversight and congressional committees are excessively simplified. Ideas for legislation may come from individuals and committees just as oversight can. On many legislative matters the voice of the congressional committee is de facto the voice of the Congress, just as it is for oversight. Also, the ability of congressmen to oversee effectively is closely linked to the threat of legislation to counter perceived executive malfeasance or nonfeasance. These and other factors weaken the force of arguments about how the Congress is not suited to legislate, but is suited to oversee.

A blending of constituent service and legislative oversight further blunts the force of Huntington's analysis: "Constituent service and legislative oversight are two sides of the same coin."[33] Most congressmen, because they are oriented toward reelection, will process constituents' cases as effectively as they can. Some constituent service is translated into legislative oversight. But that does not mean that one should equate the two. Most congressmen, the evidence suggests, seldom reflect on the general problems symbolized in each case or try to achieve anything beyond getting satisfaction for a constituent. It is this too easy mating of constituent service with legislative oversight which enables Huntington to argue the proposition that legislative oversight is the main congressional activity.

In my interviews, most congressmen and staff persons rejected the notion that their primary work is oversight. They defended their position both by calculating time spent and by assessing qualitative involvement. It is true, as argued in chapter 6, that congressmen and staff members sometimes perform oversight and do not label their acts as such. An argument that more oversight occurs than might seem to be the case is not the same as saying that oversight has become the principal activity of the Congress, although it is tempting to leap rapidly to that conclusion. Whether oversight has become the primary function of the Congress, or whether congressmen view it as such even if it has, is highly problematical. Few congressmen and staff members interviewed in 1965, 1966, and 1967 held a "bullish" attitude about the future of oversight.

The resurgence of congressional interest in supervising the bureaucracy which accompanied the scandals in the Nixon administration in the early 1970s seemed to support Huntington's analysis. These stirrings, however, should be viewed more as a transitory phenomenon than as the first step toward an enduring pattern of vigorous legislative oversight. The standard pattern has been rise and fall, not onward and upward.

Three Modest Changes

Those searching for rays of hope for improving the oversight function of the Congress will have to settle for glimmers. For example, the General Accounting Office, long an instrument of the Congress with great potential for oversight purposes but in some ways not effective in practice, has over the last decade altered its activities to provide more support for congressional units interested in oversight. This transition in the functioning of the GAO is documented in the trailblazing research by Joseph Pois, who demonstrates that the GAO has moved from a technical arm largely concerned with problems of finance to a policy arm concerned broadly with how governmental functions are performed and the conditions under which they are carried out.[34] The GAO can be an increasingly useful tool for those very few congressmen who have lacked the staff support necessary to oversee effectively.

The increasing tendency toward professionalization of congressional staffs contributes to the same end.[35] Congressional committees, as they beef up the professional staffs, can modestly raise the quality of oversight.

The easiest step that the Congress can take is to provide the resources that will enable some additional oversight to be undertaken by those who wish to do so.

Some change is also possible in the area of processing casework, where many opportunities are lost to promote oversight because congressmen simply do not choose to use them. Hundreds of cases involving alleged bureaucratic irregularities come into every congressional office every year. These numbers probably are going up. According to those who handle cases, most are seen simply as problems to be solved for the person raising the complaint; only a minority of cases became spurs to introducing legislation and/or attempting investigations.

The persistence of casework and existing congressional concern with it suggests that this might be a fruitful area in which to look for improvement in oversight. Congressmen and their office staffs are already interested in casework because they relate the efficient processing of cases to the political success of the congressmen. Since they are going to go through these motions anyway, some added attention to the implications of casework might be possible without drastic changes in the congressman's priorities or behavior. The development of greater computer capabilities in the Congress will surely facilitate taking this step.

These changes will produce a modest impact. Of the three paths that Huntington charts, the most walkable is that the Congress will continue to perform oversight in an intermittent and sporadic fashion with occasional substantial impacts and with many gaps.

The ever present possibility of oversight should continue to trigger "the law of anticipated reaction." Some would even argue that the general power to oversee is more central than any particular use of it. Stephen K. Bailey suggests that the primary value in the legislature's power to oversee lies in the potential that the power might actually be used.[36]

Some Final Reflections

Any drastic restructuring of power relationships in the Congress is tied to forces far broader than those operating within that institution itself. As argued in *The American Legislative Process*, changes in Congress are most likely to occur in response to major changes in the society as a whole or in politically crucial segments of it.[37] The Congress is an integral aspect of the political process. We should not expect the Congress to reform itself unless pressured to do so by forces and interests external to it.

For legislative oversight, member priorities are central. Congressmen, if they desire to, can frequently make the time, manipulate the structures, and create the resources to do a more extensive and effective job of overseeing. Altering their priorities is the key. Merely telling members of the Congress to do that will accomplish little. But priorities can be changed by means other than frontal assault. Manipulating structures and resources may create unforeseen feedback effects. Priorities can also be modified as members develop new interests and gain new status (such as a committee chairmanship), or as new members are elected to the Congress.

More attention to the intersections of legislative structures and member priorities is urgently needed!

If present actions are based on a shrewd assessment of political realities, then altering these realities or perceptions of them is necessary for changing behavior. Congressmen will not knowingly set priorities that contribute to their political suicide. But it is realistic to expect that, in an altered context, congressmen will act differently than they do now.

A discussion of restructuring the priorities of decision makers treads in complex and murky territory. Some members slide through their congressional careers just as other people live from day to day without much attention to what it all means and where they might be going. Most congressmen do not seem to be so passive. They try to shape their behavior to what they think is of consequence as well as in response to direct pressures on them.

Congressmen, as individuals, set their priorities in a variety of ways, but they all intend to do what they presume to be important. To the extent that oversight is connected more intimately with the central problem of political survival or with other things congressmen value, the performance of oversight will improve; to the extent that that link is seen as weak, far-fetched, or elusive, the present state of oversight will persist.

Notes

Bibliography

Index

Notes

Chapter 1. Legislative Oversight: Theory and Practice

1. *Congress and the New Politics* (Boston: Little, Brown and Company, 1969), p. 130. For similar statements, see Roger H. Davidson, David M. Kovenock, and Michael K. O'Leary, *Congress in Crisis: Politics and Congressional Reform* (Belmont, Calif.: Wadsworth Publishing Company, Inc., 1966), p. 174; Ralph K. Huitt, "The Internal Distribution of Influence: The Senate," in *The Congress and America's Future*, by the American Assembly, ed. David B. Truman (Englewood Cliffs, N.J.: Prentice-Hall, Inc., 1965), p. 94; and Dale Vinyard, "The Congressional Committees on Small Business: Pattern of Legislative Committee—Executive Agency Relations," *Western Political Quarterly*, 21, no. 3 (September 1968), pp. 391, 399.

2. "Congressional Committee Members as Independent Agency Overseers: A Case Study," *American Political Science Review*, 54, no. 4 (December 1960), p. 919.

3. James A. Robinson, *Congress and Foreign Policy—Making: A Study in Legislative Influence and Initiative.* 1st ed. (Homewood, Ill.: The Dorsey Press, Inc., 1962), p. 229.

4. V, no. 5 (January 1950), p. 22.

5. Joseph P. Harris, *Congressional Control of Administration* (Washington, D.C.: The Brookings Institution, 1964), p. 2.

6. *Bureaucracy in a Democracy* (New York: Harper & Row, 1950), p. 81.

7. Davidson, Kovenock, and O'Leary, *Congress in Crisis.*

8. Joseph P. Harris, *Congressional Control of Administration,* passim.

9. For examples, see John F. Bibby, "Committee Characteristics and Legislative Oversight of Administration," *Midwest Journal of Political Science,* 10, no. 1 (February 1966), pp. 78–98; J. Leiper Freeman, *The Political Process* (New York: Random House, 1955); Seymour

Scher, "Conditions for Legislative Control," *Journal of Politics*, 25, no. 3 (August 1963), pp. 526–51; Seymour Scher, "Congressional Committee Members," pp. 911–20; and Dale Vinyard, "Congressional Committees on Small Business," *Western Political Quarterly*, pp. 391–99.

10. (Boston: Little, Brown and Company, 1973).

11. For an example, see Dale Vinyard, "Congressional Committees on Small Business," *Midwest Journal of Political Science*, 10, no. 3 (August 1966), p. 376.

12. U.S., Congress, Joint Committee on the Organization of Congress, *Hearings on S. Con. Res. 2*, 89th Cong., 1st sess., 1965, p. 594.

13. Samuel C. Patterson related the ability of a staff to provide information more to professionalization than to size ("The Professional Staffs of Congressional Committees," *Administrative Science Quarterly*, 15, no. 1 [March 1970], p. 35).

14. "Congressional Staff and Public Policy-Making: The Joint Committee on Internal Revenue Taxation," *Journal of Politics*, 30, no. 4 (November 1968), p. 1067.

15. A useful discussion of subcommittees is found in George Goodwin, Jr., *The Little Legislatures: Committees of Congress* (Amherst: University of Massachusetts Press, 1970), pp. 45–63.

16. Robinson, *Congress and Foreign Policy–Making*, pp. 168–90.

17. (New York: McGraw-Hill Co., Inc., 1963), p. 375.

18. Richard F. Fenno, Jr., "The Impact of PPBS on the Congressional Appropriation Process," in *Information Support, Program Budgeting, and the Congress*, ed. R. L. Chartrand, K. Janda, and M. Hugo (New York: Spartan Books, 1968), pp. 181–82.

19. Quoted in Charles L. Clapp, *The Congressman: His Work as He Sees It* (Washington, D.C.: The Brookings Institution, 1963), p. 278.

20. For an example, see Thomas A. Henderson, *Congressional Oversight of Executive Agencies: A Study of the House Committee on Government Operations* (Gainesville: University of Florida Press, 1970), p. 42.

21. Press release, July 25, 1966.

22. *The Congressional Party* (New York: John Wiley & Sons, Inc., 1959), pp. 279–319.

23. *Power in the House* (New York: E. P. Dutton & Co., Inc., 1968), p. 19.

24. "Conditions for Legislative Control," pp. 528–29, 531–32.

25. Kenneth E. Gray, "Congressional Interference in Administration," in *Cooperation and Conflict*, ed. D. J. Elazar, R. B. Carroll, E. L. Levine, and D. St. Angelo (Ithaca, Ill.: F. E. Peacock Publishers, Inc., 1969), p. 525.

26. John Bibby and Roger Davidson, *On Capitol Hill* (New York: Holt, Rinehart and Winston, Inc., 1967), p. 189.

27. For example, see Ira Sharkansky, "An Appropriations Sub-committee and Its Client Agencies," *American Political Science Review*, 59, no. 3 (September 1965), p. 628.

28. For a very useful discussion of theory-building in respect to the legislative process, see Robert L. Peabody and Ralph K. Huitt, *Congress: Two Decades of Analysis* (New York: Harper and Row, Publishers, 1969), pp. 3–73.

Chapter 2. The House Post Office and Civil Service Committee

1. Another sign of inactivity is found in Gerald Cullinan's book, *The United States Postal Service*, where Chairman Tom Murray's name does not even appear in the index (New York: Frederick A. Praeger, Publishers, 1973). Another preliminary indicator of committee activity might be found in the absence of committee mentions in the daily listing entitled "The Proceedings in Washington" which appears in the *New York Times*.

2. U.S., Public Law 79–601.

3. *Pittsburgh Press*, August 9, 1967, p. 44. For a discussion of interest groups as suppliers of information, see Edward Schneier, "The Intelligence of Congress: Information and Public Policy Patterns," *The Annals*, 388 (March 1970), pp. 20–21.

4. One member, without excessive exaggeration, described Morrison's power as follows: "The best rule of thumb for this committee in the 89th Congress was: 'What Morrison wants, Morrison gets.' "

5. 2d ed., rev. (Homewood, Ill.: The Dorsey Press, 1967), pp. 161–69.

6. Transcript of television interview reprinted in *Congressional Quarterly*, July 23, 1965, p. 1434.

7. Gerald Cullinan suggests that congressional dislike for Postmaster General Arthur Summerfield contributed to his ineffectiveness. Cullinan quotes one Republican legislator who, "when told that Summerfield was really his own worst enemy . . . [replied,] 'Not while I'm alive, he isn't' " (*United States Postal Service*, p. 159).

Chapter 3. The Post Office and Civil Service Committee: Member Priorities and Oversight

1. "Correlates of Committee Transfers in the United States House of Representatives," paper prepared for the Annual Meeting of the Midwest Political Science Association, 1971, p. 3, n. 14. Some other

studies which indicate that the House Post Office and Civil Service Committee is considered one of the least desirable in the House are: James W. Dyson and John W. Soule, "Congressional Committee Behavior on Roll Call Votes: The U.S. House of Representatives, 1955–64," *Midwest Journal of Political Science*, 14, no. 4 (November 1970), pp. 633–34; and George Goodwin, Jr., "The Seniority System in Congress," *American Political Science Review*, 53, no. 2 (June 1959), p. 433.

2. "Committee Assignments in the House of Representatives," *American Political Science Review*, 55, no. 2 (June 1961), p. 353.

3. National Association of Letter Carriers, *Branch Officers' Guide* (Washington, D.C., n.d.), p. 3.

4. *New York Times*, May 1, 1967, p. 25.

5. *Progressive*, May 1966, p. 1.

6. *Union Postal Clerk*, August 1965, p. 8.

7. Ibid., p. 7.

8. Quoted in publicity release of the National Association of Letter Carriers from remarks delivered at the NALC conference, June 21, 1965.

9. *Pittsburgh Press*, July 10, 1966; emphasis added.

10. J. Edward Day, *My Appointed Round* (New York: Holt, Rinehart and Winston, 1965), p. 67.

11. Joseph Young, *Washington Evening Star*, October 18, 1965.

12. Joseph Young, *Washington Evening Star*, May 30, 1966.

13. John Cramer, *Washington Daily News*, June 16, 1965.

14. *The United States Postal Service* (New York: Frederick A. Praeger, Publishers, 1973), p. 153.

15. "Panel Puts Its Stamp On New Postal Setup," March 9, 1968, p. 128.

16. *New York Times*, May 25, 1969. The politics of the passage of the Postal Reorganization Act deserves a full study itself.

17. (Boston: Little, Brown and Company, 1973.)

18. Cullinan, *United States Postal Service*, p. 165.

19. Ibid., p. 155–56.

20. Ibid., p. 155.

Chapter 4. The Special Subcommittee on the Invasion of Privacy

1. U.S., Congress, House, Government Operations Committee, *Privacy and the National Data Bank Concept*, 90th Cong., 2d sess., 1968, H. Rept. 1842, p. 2.

2. U.S., Congress, House, Government Operations Committee, *The Computer and Invasion of Privacy*, 89th Cong., 2d sess., 1966, pp. 3, 4.

3. Ibid., p. 51.

4. U.S., Congress, House, Government Operations Committee, 89th Cong., 1st sess., 1965, p. 9.

5. For examples see the *Congressional Record*, 89th Cong., 2d sess., June 14, 1966, p. 12506 (daily edition), where Congressman Gallagher notes: "This Committee [SSIP] is a tribute to the able and distinguished Chairman of the Government Operations Committee, the honorable William Dawson, and his concern for his fellow man."

6. U.S., Congress, House, Government Operations Committee, 90th Cong,, 2d sess , 1968, p. 3.

7. The Ruggles Report is reprinted in Appendix One of the hearings entitled *The Computer and Invasion of Privacy*, p. 202.

8. Ralph L. Bisco, "Social Science Data Archives: A Review of Developments," *American Political Science Review*, 60, no. 1 (March 1966), p. 107.

9. "Data Banks and Dossiers," no. 7, p. 3.

10. *New York Times*, April 15, 1966, p. 23

11. Hearings entitled *The Computer and Invasion of Privacy*, p. 65.

12. Ibid., p. 2.

13. Ibid., p. 64.

14. Ibid., p. 103.

15. Ibid., pp. 103–04.

16. See, for examples, Jerry Martin Rosenberg, *The Death of Privacy* (New York: Random House, 1969); Alan Westin, *Privacy and Freedom* (New York: Atheneum, 1967); and Arthur R. Miller, *The Assault on Privacy* (Ann Arbor: University of Michigan Press, 1971).

17. An issue perceived as "hot" seldom fails to attract attention in the Congress. The Senate Subcommittee on Administrative Practice and Procedure held hearings in March 1967 and in February 1968. The Senate Subcommittee on Constitutional Rights held hearings during 1971.

18. Hearings entitled *The Computer and Invasion of Privacy*, p. 76.

19. Ibid., p. 131. See also pp. 120, 123.

20. Ibid., p. 4.

21. U.S., Congress, House, Government Operations Committee, *Activities of the House Government Operations Committee, Eighty-Ninth Congress*, 89th Cong., 2d sess., December 1966, committee print.

22. For example, in the hearings on personality testing held in 1965, *Special Inquiry on Invasion of Privacy.*

23. Hearings entitled *The Computer and Invasion of Privacy,* pp. 17–18.

24. January 7, 1968, p. 1.

25. Hearings entitled *Privacy and the National Data Bank Concept,* p. 21.

26. Hearings entitled *Special Inquiry on Invasion of Privacy,* p. 7.

27. Ibid., p. 2.

28. Ibid., pp. 2, 9, 301–03, 307.

29. Ibid., p. 262.

30. Ibid., p. 335.

31. Ibid., p. 106.

32. Ibid., p. 164.

33. For samples of how this process operates, see ibid., pp. 38–39, 43–46, 292, 303, 323.

34. Ibid., p. 51.

35. Ibid., pp. 231, 232, 237–38.

36. Ibid., pp. 91–92, 105, 221, 302–03.

37. Ibid., p. 353.

38. U.S., Congress, Senate, Committee on the Judiciary, *Psychological Tests and Constitutional Rights,* 89th Cong., 1st sess., 1965, p. 169.

39. *Congressional Record,* 88th Cong., 2d sess., May 7, 1964, p. 10397.

40. "The 1965 Congressional Inquiry Into Testing," 20, no. 11 (November 1965), p. 863.

41. Hearings entitled *Psychological Tests and Constitutional Rights,* p. 144.

42. Ibid., p. 207.

43. Hearings entitled *Special Inquiry on Invasion of Privacy,* p. 39.

44. Ibid., p. 44.

45. Hearings entitled *Psychological Tests and Constitutional Rights,* pp. 207–08.

46. In 1973 the press reported that Congressman Gallagher had pleaded guilty to charges of perjury, conspiracy, and tax evasion. He was subsequently sentenced to a two-year jail term. These events took place long after the interviewing and analysis for this chapter were completed. Subsequent reinterviewing uncovered no evidence that would suggest alternative analyses of the SSIP.

Chapter 5. The House Judiciary Committee: Subcommittee Five

1. U.S., Congress, House, Rules Committee, *Policies and Guidelines for School Desegregation*, 89th Cong., 2d sess., 1966, p. 16. In the 89th Congress particularly, the Judiciary Committee received 35.8 percent of all measures introduced in the House.

2. Subcommittee Five in the 89th Congress had 453 bills referred to it and held hearings on 371 of them (*Legislative Calendar, Committee on the Judiciary*, 89th Cong., 1966, pp. 9, 18).

3. *Washington Post*, February 2, 1969.

4. In the 89th Congress, 66 percent of the House Judiciary Committee members had single committee assignments. By contrast, only 12 percent of the members of the House Post Office and Civil Service Committee had a single assignment (Louis C. Gawthrop, "Changing Membership Patterns in House Committees," *American Political Science Review*, 60, no. 2 [June 1966], p. 367).

5. Despite the priority given to the subcommittee by interviewees in 1965 and 1966, by 1971 seven of the eleven members of the subcommittee were no longer members. The limits of the case study can be severe.

6. For a complete list, see *Congressional Record*, 89th Cong., 2d sess., September 21, 1966, pp. 22547–48 (daily edition).

7. Ibid.

8. Ibid., pp. 22545–48.

9. Ibid., p. 22547.

10. U.S., Public Law 88–352.

11. Ibid.

12. U.S., Congress, House, Committee on the Judiciary, *Guidelines for School Desegregation*, 89th Cong., 2d sess., 1966, p. 22.

13. Hearings entitled *Policies and Guidelines for School Desegregation*, p. 16.

14. Ibid., p. 6.

15. In hearings conducted by Judiciary Subcommittee Five in 1966 on miscellaneous proposals concerning civil rights, some 61 of 1,765 pages contained material dealing with questions of oversight.

Chapter 6. Oversight as a Latent and a Manifest Function

1. George B. Galloway, *History of the House of Representatives* (New York: Thomas Y. Crowell Company, 1961), p. 9.

2. Malcolm E. Jewell and Samuel C. Patterson, *The Legislative Process in the United States* (New York: Random House, 1966), pp. 454–55; see also pp. 454–61.

3. William J. Keefe and Morris S. Ogul, *The American Legislative Process* (Englewood Cliffs, N.J.: Prentice-Hall, Inc., 1973), p. 206.

4. For examples, see Arlen Large, "Congressional Hearings," *Wall Street Journal*, August 25, 1966, p. 12, and Nan Robertson, "House Hearing: Its Ritual and Reality," *New York Times*, August 21, 1967, p. 1.

5. U.S., Congress, House, Appropriations Committee, *Hearings on Treasury—Post Office Departments and Executive Office Appropriations for 1966*, 89th Cong., 1st sess., 1965, p. 405.

6. Ibid., p. 89.

7. *New York Times*, February 24, 1967, p. 33.

8. Of forty-four interviews where legislators or staff members made general comments about the utility of hearings for oversight, eleven explicitly used the term "window-dressing." In only one interview did the respondent assert that legislative hearings were crucial as oversight activity.

9. Alan Rosenthal reports that in the Maryland legislature, "only two out of five members feel that committee hearings serve to help the legislature keep track of programs being administered by the executive" (*Strengthening the Maryland Legislature* [New Brunswick, N.J.: Rutgers University Press, 1968], p. 53).

10. For an interesting discussion of related points, see Edward Schneier, "The Intelligence of Congress: Information and Public Policy Patterns," *The Annals*, 388 (March 1970), esp. pp. 19–20.

11. For some fragmentary data, see Lowell H. Hattery and Susan Hofheimer, "The Legislator's Source of Expert Information," *Public Opinion Quarterly*, 18, no. 3 (Fall 1954), pp. 300–03.

12. *The Political Process: Executive Bureau—Legislative Committee Relations*, (New York: Random House, 1965), pp. 82, 123.

13. For a related statement, see Thomas A. Henderson, *Congressional Oversight of Executive Agencies: A Study of the House Committee on Government Operations* (Gainesville: University of Florida Press, 1970), p. 40.

14. For other examples, see the comments of Representative Henry S. Reuss (D.–Wisconsin) as reported in the *New York Times*, June 5, 1966, concerning federal grants to a wealthy suburban school district. See also Kenneth E. Gray, "Congressional Interference in Administration," paper prepared for the 1962 meeting of the American Political Science Association, p. 7.

15. Huitt suggests that "most legislative oversight occurs when

hearings on new bills or authorizations occur" ("Congress the Durable Partner," in *Lawmakers in a Changing World,* ed. Elke Frank [Englewood Cliffs, N.J.: Prentice-Hall, Inc., 1966], p. 20). If oversight occurs in these hearings as seldom as it seems to, Huitt's judgment speaks very loudly about the condition of legislative oversight generally.

16. Legislative casework is defined as the attempt by members of the Congress to assist their constituents, in response to requests, in dealing with the bureaucracy.

17. *The Congressman: His Work as He Sees It* (Washington, D.C.: The Brookings Institution, 1963), pp. 51, 52, 55.

18. *Congress in Crisis: Politics and Congressional Reform* (Belmont, Calif.: Wadsworth Publishing Company, Inc., 1966), p. 77.

19. George B. Galloway, *The Legislative Process in Congress* (New York: Thomas Y. Crowell Company, 1953), p. 203.

20. Donald R. Matthews, *U.S. Senators and Their World* (Chapel Hill: University of North Carolina Press, 1960), p. 227. Charles Clapp, citing a member's statement, suggests that casework may have therapeutic value for some congressmen (*The Congressman,* p. 106).

21. Kenneth G. Olson, "The Service Function of the United States Congress," in *Congress: The First Branch of Government,* ed. Alfred de Grazia (Washington, D.C.: The American Enterprise Institute for Public Policy Research, 1966), pp. 324–25.

22. Joseph S. Clark, *Congress: The Sapless Branch* (New York: Harper & Row, Publishers, 1964), pp. 63–64.

23. Joe L. Evins, *Understanding Congress* (New York: Clarkson N. Potter, Inc., 1963), p. 42. See also Kenneth E. Gray, "Congressional Interference in Administration," probably the best single discussion of the positive contributions of casework to the legislative process.

24. Walter Gellhorn, *When Americans Complain: Governmental Grievance Procedures* (Cambridge: Harvard University Press, 1966), p. 63. Morris K. Udall and Donald G. Tacheron report that in a survey of 158 congressmen conducted by John Saloma under the auspices of The Study of Congress, the breakdown of the use of a week's time revealed 8.6 percent spent handling constituent problems and 12.1 percent spent answering mail. An average mail count per week was 521 pieces, 64 of which involved casework. Whether a crucial function or errand-running was being performed, the subject requires more attention (*The Job of the Congressman* [Indianapolis, Ind.: Bobbs-Merrill Company, Inc., 1966], pp. 280–82).

25. See especially Clapp, *The Congressman,* pp. 78–80.

26. *Congress and Foreign Policy–Making: A Study in Legislative Influence and Initiative,* 2d ed., rev. (Homewood, Ill.: The Dorsey Press, 1967), p. 149.

27. *Congressional Record,* 89th Cong., 1st sess., 1965, p. 2489.

28. Robinson, *Congress and Foreign Policy–Making,* p. 164.

29. Ibid., p. 162.

30. U.S., Congress, House, Government Operations Committee, *Special Inquiry on Invasion of Privacy,* 89th Cong., 1st sess., 1965, p. 271.

31. Olson, "Service Function," p. 360.

32. U.S., Congress, Senate, Committee on the Judiciary, *Psychological Tests and Constitutional Rights,* 89th Cong., 1st sess., 1965, p. 1.

33. *New York Times,* April 14, 1965, p. 35.

34. April 1, 1967.

35. *Hearings on Treasury–Post Office Departments,* p. 125. Cf. Gellhorn, *When Americans Complain,* p. 114.

36. *My Appointed Round* (New York: Holt, Rinehart and Winston, 1965), p. 19.

37. For an example involving parcel post, see Gellhorn, *When Americans Complain,* p. 108.

38. *Pittsburgh Press,* August 24, 1966, p. 33.

39. Robert G. Sherrill, "Rebels on the Potomac," *Nation,* February 27, 1967, pp. 265–68.

40. *New York Times,* August 23, 1969, p. 10.

41. *Congressional Record,* 78th Cong., 1st sess., 1943, pp. A2250–51.

42. "Congressmen as Washington Agents for Constituents," *Business and Government Review,* 8, no. 5 (September–October 1967), p. 24.

43. "Administrative Accountability: Reporting to Congress," *Western Political Quarterly,* 10, no. 2 (June 1957), pp. 405–15.

44. U.S., Congress, Joint Committee on the Organization of Congress, *Final Report,* pursuant to S. Con. Res. 2, 1966, 89th Cong., 2d sess., p. 25.

45. "Congress and the Executive," paper prepared for the 1962 annual meetings of the American Political Science Association, p. 10.

46. The research of John Johannes adds considerably to the analysis available. His forthcoming articles will prove to be useful complements to the research by Smith and Cotter.

47. *Final Report,* p. 25.

48. Another area that might be fruitful to study is the impact of committee recommendations in reports accompanying pieces of legislation. There are suggestions that these reports are carefully heeded by the executive departments. See Clapp, *The Congressman,* p. 270; Richard F. Fenno, Jr., *The Power of the Purse: Appropriations Politics in*

Congress (Boston: Little, Brown and Company, 1966), pp. 18 ff. See also Michael W. Kirst, *Government Without Passing Laws: Congress' Non-Statutory Techniques for Appropriations Control* (Chapel Hill: University of North Carolina Press, 1969).

Chapter 7. Legislative Oversight in the Present and in the Future

1. The interviewing for this study was conducted in 1965 and 1966, when the literature on legislative oversight was modest. Since then, studies about legislative oversight have appeared more frequently. Fortunately my findings, although independently derived, substantially square with those emerging from other research.

2. For similar findings, see Seymour Scher, "Conditions for Legislative Control," *Journal of Politics*, 25, no. 3 (August 1963), p. 530; and Thomas A. Henderson, *Congressional Oversight of Executive Agencies: A Study of the House Committee on Government Operations* (Gainesville: University of Florida Press, 1970), p. 13.

3. Scher, "Conditions for Legislative Control," p. 530. See also Hendersen, *Congressional Oversight*, p. 13; and Seymour Scher, "Congressional Committee Members as Independent Agency Overseers: A Case Study," *American Political Science Review*, 54, no. 4 (December 1960), p. 920.

4. *Professional Staffs of Congress* (West Lafayette, Ind.: Purdue University Press, 1962), p. 145.

5. "Committee Characteristics and Legislative Oversight of Administration," *Midwest Journal of Political Science*, 10, no. 1 (February 1966), p. 98. See also Scher, "Conditions for Legislative Control," p. 531; and John S. Saloma, III, *Congress and the New Politics* (Boston: Little, Brown and Company, 1969), p. 153.

6. See also Richard F. Fenno, Jr., *The Power of the Purse: Appropriations Politics in Congress* (Boston: Little, Brown and Company, 1966), p. 286.

7. See also Scher, "Conditions for Legislative Control," p. 541; John F. Bibby, "Congressional Committee Oversight of Administration: The Impact of External Conditions," mimeographed paper (1966), p. 20; and Joseph P. Harris, *Congressional Control of Administration* (Washington, D.C.: The Brookings Institution, 1964), pp. 292–93.

8. Scher, "Conditions for Legislative Control," p. 531.

9. For this same point see Ralph K. Huitt, "The Internal Distribution of Influence: The Senate," in *The Congress and America's Future*, by the American Assembly, ed. David B. Truman (Englewood Cliffs,

N.J.: Prentice-Hall, Inc., 1965), p. 94. See also Dale Vinyard, "The Congressional Committees on Small Business: Pattern of Legislative Committee—Executive Agency Relations," *Western Political Quarterly*, 21, no. 3 (September 1968), pp. 398–99.

10. *The Administration of National Economic Control* (New York: The Macmillan Company, 1952; reprint ed., Johnson Reprint Corp., 1971), p. 352.

11. See Huitt, "Internal Distribution of Influence," p. 94. The variation in committee behavior is a central theme in Richard F. Fenno, Jr., *Congressmen in Committees* (Boston: Little, Brown and Company, 1973). See also Dale Vinyard, "Congressional Committees on Small Business," *Western Political Quarterly*, p. 399, and "Congressional Checking on Executive Agencies," *Business and Government Review*, 2, no. 5 (September—October 1970), pp. 15, 17. Vinyard suggests three patterns of committee oversight. The evidence herein provides an example of each pattern.

12. *The Political Process: Executive Bureau—Legislative Committee Relations* (New York: Random House, 1955), p. 65. For some statements agreeing, see Bibby, "Committee Characteristics," p. 97; Vinyard, "Congressional Committees on Small Business," *Western Political Quarterly*, p. 398; and Huitt, "Internal Distribution of Influence," p. 94.

13. For a similar point, see Kofmehl, *Professional Staffs*, pp. 205, 207.

14. For other examples see Freeman, *Political Process*, p. 66; MacAlister Brown, "The Demise of State Department Public Opinion Polls: A Study in Legislative Oversight," *Midwest Journal of Political Science*, 5, no. 1 (February 1961), pp. 1–17.

15. "Congress the Durable Partner," in *Lawmakers in a Changing World*, ed. Elke Frank (Englewood Cliffs, N.J.: Prentice-Hall, Inc., 1966), p. 20. See also R. L. Chartrand, K. Janda, and M. Hugo, eds., *Information Support, Program Budgeting, and the Congress* (New York: Spartan Books, 1968), p. 142; Redford, *Administration of National Economic Control*, p. 306; and Vinyard, "Congressional Committees on Small Business," *Western Political Quarterly*, p. 399.

16. For some attention to the informal dimensions of oversight see Vinyard, "Congressional Checking," pp. 15–17; Vinyard, "Congressional Committees on Small Business," *Western Political Quarterly*, p. 399; and Scher, "Conditions for Legislative Control," p. 534. See also Redford, *Administration of National Economic Control*, pp. 350–51; and Bibby, "Congressional Committee Oversight," pp. 5, 14.

17. U.S., Congress, 93rd Cong., 2d sess., House Resolution 988.

18. *Congress in Crisis: Politics and Congressional Reform* (Belmont, Calif.: Wadsworth Publishing Company, Inc., 1966), p. 174.

19. U.S., Congress, Joint Committee on the Organization of Congress, *Hearings Pursuant to S. Con. Res. 2,* 89th Cong., 1st sess., 1965, p. 780.

20. U.S., Public Law 91-510. H. Res. 988, passed in the 93rd Congress, 2d session, further elaborates the oversight authority of committees in the House of Representatives.

21. *Hearings Pursuant to S. Con. Res. 2,* p. 779.

22. "The Concept of Legislative Oversight," in *Congress: The First Branch of Government,* ed. Alfred de Grazia (Washington, D.C.: The American Enterprise Institute for Public Policy Research, 1966), p. 81.

23. For a useful analysis of the problems in thinking about administrative responsibility, see Charles E. Gilbert, "The Framework of Administrative Responsibility," *Journal of Politics,* 21, no. 3 (August 1959), pp. 373–407.

24. For Friedrich's statement about how to enforce administrative responsibility, see his *Constitutional Government and Democracy* (Boston: Ginn and Company, 1950), pp. 398–99.

25. The research in this book is based on interviews with thirty-four congressmen, thirty-eight staff members, five spokesmen for interest groups, and twelve other knowledgeable persons, including ten at the level of assistant secretary or above in the executive branch. Beyond the interviews, committee documents for the relevant period were perused and the atmosphere of committee operations was absorbed in an osmosislike fashion simply by extensive "hanging around" and by talking informally to people. In the abstract, the weight of this data base is slight; in fact, it does add a sizable increment to what is published about legislative oversight.

26. The address was printed as "Congressional Control of the Public Service," *American Political Science Review,* 39, no. 1 (February 1945), pp. 1–11. Professor White's comments would not have seemed out of place in the hearings on oversight held by the House Select Committee on Committees in 1973.

27. See, for example, Samuel P. Huntington, "Congressional Responses to the Twentieth Century," in *The Congress and America's Future,* by the American Assembly, ed. David B. Truman (Englewood Cliffs, N.J.: Prentice-Hall, Inc., 1965), p. 25.

28. See, for example, Donald H. Riddle, *The Truman Committee: A Study in Congressional Responsibility* (New Brunswick, N.J.: Rutgers University Press, 1964).

29. "Congressional Responses," pp. 5–31.

30. Ibid., p. 26.

31. Ibid.

32. Ibid., p. 30.

33. Ibid., p. 25.

34. Professor Pois was kind enough to allow me to read an early draft of his manuscript tentatively titled "Watchdog on the Potomac." His first published product of this research is "Trends in General Accounting Office Audits," in *The New Political Economy: The Public Use of the Private Sector*, ed. Bruce L. R. Smith (London: The Macmillan Press, Ltd., 1975), pp. 245–77. See also section 702 of the Congressional Budget and Impoundment Control Act of 1974 (P.L. 93-344), which spells out some GAO functions to be performed for the Congress.

35. The best discussion of this point is in Samuel C. Patterson, "The Professional Staffs of Congressional Committees," *Administrative Science Quarterly*, 15, no. 1 (March 1970), pp. 22–37.

36. See *The New Congress* (New York: St. Martin's Press, 1966), pp. 85, 90.

37. William J. Keefe and Morris S. Ogul, 3d ed. (Englewood Cliffs, N.J.: Prentice-Hall, Inc., 1973), see esp. chap. 14.

Bibliography

This book is based mainly on interviews with members of Congress, their staffs, officials in the executive branch, and spokesmen for interest groups. The written sources used are cited in the footnotes and, where sizable sections of a work are closely related to the study of oversight, listed below. This bibliography offers a substantial list of sources useful for the study of legislative oversight of bureaucracy. The emphasis is on published books and articles. The aim is not inclusiveness, but utility.

Many sources touch on oversight as other aspects of the legislative process are discussed. Major research on Congress is synthesized in William J. Keefe and Morris S. Ogul, *The American Legislative Process* (1973), Malcolm E. Jewell and Samuel C. Patterson, *The Legislative Process in the United States* (1973), and Leroy N. Rieselbach, *Congressional Politics* (1973). Therefore, a general list of sources on the legislative process need not be provided here.

Books Related to the Study of Legislative Oversight

Barth, Alan. *Government by Investigation*. New York: Viking Press, 1955.

Berger, Raoul. *Executive Privilege: A Constitutional Myth*. Cambridge: Harvard University Press, 1974.

Bibby, John F. "Congress' Neglected Function." In *Republican Papers*, edited by Melvin R. Laird, pp. 477—88. New York: F. A. Praeger, 1968.

Brown, Richard E. *The GAO: Untapped Source of Congressional Power*. Knoxville: University of Tennessee Press, 1970.

Carr, Robert K. *The House Committee on Un-American Activities, 1945—1950*. Ithaca, N.Y.: Cornell University Press, 1952.

Carroll, Holbert N. "The Congress and National Security Policy." In *The Congress and America's Future*, by the American Assembly, edited by David B. Truman, pp. 179–201. Englewood Cliffs, N.J.: Prentice-Hall Inc., 1965.

_____. *The House of Representatives and Foreign Affairs*. Revised edition. Boston: Little, Brown and Co., 1966.

Clapp, Charles L. *The Congressman: His Work as He Sees It*. Washington, D.C.: The Brookings Institution, 1963.

Cooper, Joseph. "The Legislative Veto: Its Promise and Its Perils." In *Public Policy, 1956*, pp. 128–74. Cambridge, Mass.: Graduate School of Public Administration, Harvard University, 1957.

_____. *The Origins of the Standing Committees and the Development of the Modern House*. Houston, Texas: William Marsh Rice University, Monograph in Political Science 56, 1971.

Cotter, Cornelius P. "The Concept of Legislative Oversight." In *Congress: The First Branch of Government*, edited by Alfred de Grazia, pp. 24–79. Washington, D.C.: The American Enterprise Institute for Public Policy Research, 1966.

Dahl, Robert A. *Congress and Foreign Policy*. New York: Harcourt, Brace and Company, 1950.

Davidson, Roger H., Kovenock, David M., and O'Leary, Michael K. *Congress in Crisis: Politics and Congressional Reform*. Belmont, Calif.: Wadsworth Publishing Company, Inc., 1966.

Dexter, Lewis Anthony. "Congressmen and the Making of Military Policy." In *New Perspectives on the House of Representatives*, edited by Robert L. Peabody and Nelson W. Polsby, pp. 175–94. Second edition. Chicago: Rand McNally, 1969.

Dimock, Marshall E. *Congressional Investigating Committees*. Baltimore: The Johns Hopkins Press, 1929.

Doubleday, D. Jay. *Legislative Review of the Budget in California*. Berkeley: University of California, Institute of Governmental Studies, 1967.

Eberling, Ernest J. *Congressional Investigations*. New York: Columbia University Press, 1928.

Farnsworth, David N. *The Senate Committee on Foreign Relations*. Urbana: University of Illinois Press, 1961.

Fenno, Richard F., Jr. *Congressmen in Committees*. Boston: Little, Brown and Company, 1973.

_____. "The Impact of PPBS on the Congressional Appropriation Process." In *Information Support, Program Budgeting, and the Congress*, edited by R. L. Chartrand, K. Janda, and M. Hugo. New York: Spartan Books, 1968.

_____. *The Power of the Purse: Appropriations Politics in Congress.* Boston: Little, Brown and Company, 1966.

Fisher, Louis. *President and Congress: Power and Policy.* New York: The Free Press, 1972.

_____. *Presidential Spending Power.* Princeton, N.J.: Princeton University Press, scheduled for publication in 1975.

Freeman, J. Leiper. *The Political Process: Executive Bureau–Legislative Committee Relations.* Revised edition. New York: Random House, 1965.

Gellhorn, Walter. *When Americans Complain: Governmental Grievance Procedures.* Cambridge: Harvard University Press, 1966.

Goodwin, George, Jr. *The Little Legislatures: Committees of Congress.* Amherst: University of Massachusetts Press, 1970.

Gray, Kenneth E. "Congressional Interference in Administration." In *Cooperation and Conflict,* edited by D. J. Elazar, R. B. Carroll, E. L. Levine, and D. St. Angelo, pp. 521–42. Ithaca, Ill.: F. E. Peacock Publishers, Inc., 1969.

Green, Harold P., and Rosenthal, Alan. *Government of the Atom: The Integration of Power.* New York: Atherton Press, 1963.

Harris, Joseph P. *The Advice and Consent of the Senate.* Berkeley: University of California Press, 1953.

_____. *Congressional Control of Administration.* Washington, D.C.: The Brookings Institution, 1964.

Henderson, Thomas A. *Congressional Oversight of Executive Agencies: A Study of the House Committee on Government Operations.* Gainesville, Fla.: University of Florida Press, 1970.

Horn, Stephen. *Unused Power: The Work of the Senate Committee on Appropriations.* Washington, D.C.: The Brookings Institution, 1970.

Huntington, Samuel P. *The Common Defense: Strategic Programs in National Politics.* New York: Columbia University Press, 1961.

Huzar, Elias. *The Purse and the Sword: Control of Army by Congress Through Military Appropriations, 1933–1950.* Ithaca, N.Y.: Cornell University Press, 1950.

Hyneman, Charles S. *Bureaucracy in a Democracy.* New York: Harper & Row, 1950.

Key, V. O. "Legislative Control." In *Elements of Public Administration.* Edited by Fritz Morstein Marx, pp. 312–33. Englewood Cliffs, N.J.: Prentice-Hall, Inc., 1959.

Kirst, Michael W. *Government Without Passing Laws: Congress' Non-Statutory Techniques for Appropriations Control.* Chapel Hill: University of North Carolina Press, 1969.

Kofmehl, Kenneth. *Professional Staffs of Congress.* West Lafayette, Ind.: Purdue University Press, 1962.

Kolodziej, Edward A. *The Uncommon Defense and Congress, 1945–1963.* Columbus: Ohio State University Press, 1966.

Kraines, Oscar. *Congress and the Challenge of Big Government.* New York: Bookman Associates, 1958.

Maass, Arthur. *Muddy Waters: The Army Engineers and the Nation's Rivers.* Cambridge: Harvard University Press, 1951.

Manley, John F. *The Politics of Finance: The House Committee on Ways and Means.* Boston: Little, Brown and Co., 1970.

Mayhew, David R. *Congress: The Electoral Connection.* New Haven: Yale University Press, 1974.

McGeary, M. Nelson. *The Development of Congressional Investigative Power.* New York: Octagon Books, Inc., 1966.

Mollenhoff, Clark R. *The Pentagon: Politics, Profits and Plunder.* New York: Putnam, 1967.

Morrow, William L. *Congressional Committees.* New York: Charles Scribner's Sons, 1969.

Niskanen, William A., Jr. *Bureaucracy and Representative Government.* Chicago: Aldine-Atherton, 1971.

Olson, Kenneth G. "The Service Function of the United States Congress." In *Congress: The First Branch of Government,* edited by Alfred de Grazia. pp. 323–64. Washington, D.C.: The American Enterprise Institute for Public Policy Research, 1966.

Pois, Joseph. "Trends in General Accounting Office Audits." In *The New Political Economy: The Public Use of the Private Sector,* edited by Bruce L. R. Smith. London: The Macmillan Press, Ltd., 1975.

Redford, Emmette S. *The Administration of National Economic Control.* New York: The Macmillan Company, 1952. Reprinted by Johnson Reprint Corporation, 1971.

Rhode, William E. *Committee Clearance of Administrative Decisions.* East Lansing: Bureau of Social and Political Research, Michigan State University, College of Business and Public Service, 1959.

Riddle, Donald H. *The Truman Committee: A Study in Congressional Responsibility.* New Brunswick, N.J.: Rutgers University Press, 1964.

Robinson, James A. *Congress and Foreign Policy—Making: A Study in Legislative Influence and Initiative.* 2d ed., revised. Homewood, Ill.: Dorsey Press, 1967.

Rourke, Francis E. *Secrecy and Publicity.* Baltimore: Johns Hopkins Press, 1967.

Saloma, John S., III. *Congress and the New Politics.* Boston: Little, Brown and Company, 1969.

_____. *The Responsible Use of Power: A Critical Analysis of the Congressional Budget Process.* Washington, D.C.: American Enterprise Institute for Public Policy Research, 1964.

Schauffler, Peter. "The Legislative Veto Revisited." In *Public Policy, 1958,* pp. 296–327. Cambridge: Graduate School of Public Administration, Harvard University, 1958. See reply by Joseph Cooper, pp. 328–35.

Schwartz, Bernard. *The Professor and the Commissions.* New York: Knopf Publishing Company, 1959.

Shils, Edward A. *The Torment of Secrecy: The Background and Consequences of American Security Policies.* Glencoe, Ill.: The Free Press, 1956.

Smithies, Arthur. *The Budgetary Process in the United States.* New York: McGraw-Hill Book Company, Inc., 1955.

Taylor, Telford. *Grand Inquest: The Story of Congressional Investigations.* New York: Simon and Schuster, 1955.

Wallace, Robert A. *Congressional Control of Federal Spending.* Detroit: Wayne State University Press, 1960.

Wildavsky, Aaron. *The Politics of the Budgetary Process.* Boston: Little, Brown and Co., 1964.

Williams, J. D. *The Impounding of Funds by the Bureau of the Budget.* ICP Case Series no. 28. University: University of Alabama Press, 1955.

Wilmerding, Lucius. *The Spending Power: A History of the Efforts of Congress to Control Expenditures.* New Haven: Yale University Press, 1943.

Articles Related to the Study of Legislative Oversight

Baldwin, David A. "Congressional Initiative in Foreign Policy." *Journal of Politics.* 28 (November 1966):754–73.

Banfield, Edward. "Congress and the Budget: A Planner's Criticisms." *American Political Science Review.* 43 (December 1949):1217–28.

Baskir, L. M. "Reflections on the Senate Investigation of Army Surveillance." *Indiana Law Journal.* 49 (Summer 1974):618–53.

Berger, Raoul. "Executive Privilege v. Congressional Inquiry." *UCLA Law Review.* 12 (May and August 1965):1044–1120 and 1288–1364.

Bibby, John F. "Committee Characteristics and Legislative Oversight of Administration." *Midwest Journal of Political Science.* 10 (February 1966):78–98.

Borchardt, Kurt. "Congressional Use of Administration Organization and Procedure for Policy-Making Purposes: Six Case Studies and Some Conclusions." *George Washington Law Review.* 30 (March 1962):429–66.

Brown, Ben H., Jr. "Congress and the Department of State." *Annals of the American Academy of Political and Social Science.* 289 (September 1953):100–07.

Brown, McAlister. "The Demise of State Department Public Opinion Polls: A Study in Legislative Oversight." *Midwest Journal of Political Science.* 5 (February 1961):1–17.

Buckwalter, Doyle W. "The Congressional Concurrent Resolution: A Search for Foreign Policy Influence." *Midwest Journal of Political Science.* 14 (August 1970):434–58.

Burt, William C., and Kennedy, William F. "Congressional Review of Price Control." *University of Pennsylvania Law Review.* 101 (December 1952):333–77.

Carr, Robert K. "Investigations in Operation: The Un-American Activities Committee." *University of Chicago Law Review.* 18 (Spring 1951): 598–633.

Cobb, Stephen A. "Defense Spending and Foreign Policy in the House of Representatives." *Journal of Conflict Resolution.* 13 (September 1969):358–69.

Cook, Donald C. "Investigations in Operation: Senate Preparedness Subcommittee." *University of Chicago Law Review.* 18 (Spring 1951):634–46.

Cooper, Joseph, and Cooper, Ann. "The Legislative Veto and the Constitution." *George Washington Law Review.* 30 (March 1962):467–516.

Cotter, Cornelius P., and Smith, J. Malcolm. "Administrative Accountability to Congress: The Concurrent Resolution." *Western Political Quarterly.* 9 (December 1956):955–66.

_____. "Administrative Responsibility: Congressional Prescription of Inter-agency Relationships." *Western Political Quarterly.* 10 (December 1957):765–82.

Davis, Gerald W. "Congressional Power to Require Defense Expenditures." *Fordham Law Review.* 33 (October 1964):39–60.

Dawson, Raymond H. "Congressional Innovation and Intervention in Defense Policy: Legislative Authorization of Weapons Systems." *American Political Science Review.* 56 (March 1962):42–57.

Dilliard, Irving. "Congressional Investigations: The Role of the Press." *University of Chicago Law Review.* 18 (Spring 1951):585—90.

Fenno, Richard F., Jr. "The House Appropriations Committee as a Political System: The Problem of Integration." *American Political Science Review.* 56 (June 1962):310—24.

Fisher, Louis. "Funds Impounded by the President: The Constitutional Issue." *The George Washington Law Review.* 38 (October 1969):124—37.

_____. "Impoundment of Funds: Uses and Abuses." *Buffalo Law Review.* 23 (Fall 1973):141—200.

_____. "The Politics of Impounded Funds." *Administrative Science Quarterly.* 15 (September 1970):361—77.

_____. "Presidential Spending Discretion and Congressional Controls." *Law and Contemporary Problems.* 37 (Winter 1972):135—72.

_____. "Reprogramming of Funds by the Defense Department." *Journal of Politics.* 36 (Feburary 1974):77—102.

Fowler, Dorothy Ganfield. "Congressional Dictation of Local Appointments." *Journal of Politics.* 7 (February 1945):25—57.

Fulbright, J. W. "Congressional Investigations: Significance for Legislative Process." *University of Chicago Law Review.* 18 (Spring 1951):440—48.

Galloway, George B. "Congressional Investigations: Proposed Reforms." *University of Chicago Law Review.* 18 (Spring 1951):478—502.

Gilbert, Charles E. "The Framework of Administrative Responsibility." *Journal of Politics.* 21 (August 1959):373—407.

Ginnane, Robert W. "The Control of Federal Administration by Congressional Resolutions and Committees." *Harvard Law Review.* 66 (February 1953):569—611.

Gordon, Bernard K. "The Military Budget: Congressional Phase." *Journal of Politics.* 23 (November 1961):689—710.

Harris, Joseph P. "Legislative Control of Administration: Some Comparisons of American and European Practice." *Western Political Quarterly.* 10 (June 1957):465—67.

_____. "The Senatorial Rejection of Leland Olds: A Case Study." *American Political Science Review.* 45 (September 1951):674—92.

Hilsman, Roger. "Congressional-Executive Relations and the Foreign Policy Consensus." *American Political Science Review.* 52 (September 1958):725—44.

Huitt, Ralph K. "The Congressional Committee: A Case Study." *American Political Science Review.* 48 (June 1954):340—65.

Huzar, Elias. "Legislative Control Over Administration: Congress and the WPA." *American Political Science Review.* 36 (February 1942):51–67.

Jahnige, Thomas P. "The Congressional Committee System and the Oversight Process: Congress and NASA." *Western Political Quarterly.* 21 (June 1968):227–39.

James, Louis C. "Senatorial Rejections of Presidential Nominations to the Cabinet: A Study in Constitutional Custom." *Arizona Law Review.* 3 (Winter 1961):232–61.

Javits, J. K. "The Congressional Presence in Foreign Relations." *Foreign Affairs.* 48 (January 1970):221–34.

Jones, Charles O. "Representation in Congress: The Case of the House Agriculture Committee." *American Political Science Review.* 55 (June 1961):358–67.

_____. "The Role of the Congressional Subcommittee." *Midwest Journal of Political Science.* 6 (November 1962):327–44.

Kammerer, Gladys M. "Legislative Oversight of Administration in Kentucky." *Public Administration Review.* 10 (Summer 1950):169–75.

Kampelman, Max M. "Congressional Control vs. Executive Flexibility." *Public Administration Review.* 18 (Summer 1958):185–88.

Kerr, James R. "Congress and Space: Overview or Oversight?" *Public Administration Review.* 25 (September 1965):185–92.

Kim, Sun Kil. "The Politics of a Congressional Budgetary Process: 'Backdoor Spending.'" *Western Political Quarterly.* 21 (December 1968):606–23.

Kingdon, John W. "A House Appropriations Subcommittee: Influences on Budgetary Decisions." *The Southwestern Social Science Quarterly.* 47 (June 1966):68–77.

Knapp, David C. "Congressional Control of Agricultural Conservation Policy: A Case Study of the Appropriations Process." *Political Science Quarterly.* 71 (June 1956):257–81.

Kolodziej, Edward A. "Congress and Foreign Policy: Through the Looking Glass." *Virginia Quarterly Review.* 42 (Winter 1966):12–27.

_____. "Congressional Responsibility for the Common Defense: The Money Problem." *Western Political Quarterly.* 16 (March 1963): 149–60.

_____. "Rational Consent and Defense Budgets: The Role of Congress, 1945–1962." *Orbis.* 7 (Winter 1964):748–77.

Kraines, Oscar. "The President Versus Congress: The Keep Commission, 1905–1909: First Comprehensive Presidential Inquiry Into Administration." *Western Political Quarterly.* 23 (March 1970):5–54.

Kramer, Robert, and Marcuse, Herman. "Executive Privilege: A Study of the Period 1953–1960." *George Washington Law Review.* 29 (April and June 1961):623–717 and 827–916.

LaFollette, Robert M., Jr. "Systematizing Congressional Control." *American Political Science Review.* 41 (February 1947):58–68.

Leigh, Robert D. "Politicians vs. Bureaucrats: The Case of FCC Chairman Fly and Congressman Cox." *Harper's.* 190 (January 1945): 97–105.

MacMahon, Arthur. "Congressional Oversight of Administration: The Power of the Purse." *Political Science Quarterly.* 58 (June and September 1943):161–90 and 380–414.

Manley, John F. "Congressional Staff and Public Policy-Making: The Joint Committee on Internal Revenue Taxation." *Journal of Politics.* 30 (November 1968):1046–67.

Mansfield, Harvey C. "The Legislative Veto and the Deportation of Aliens." *Public Administration Review.* 1 (Spring 1941):281–86.

Marvin, Keith E., and Hedrick, James L. "GAO Helps Congress Evaluate Programs." *Public Administration Review.* 34 (July/August 1974):327–32.

McGeary, M. Nelson. "Congressional Investigations: Historical Development." *University of Chicago Law Review.* 18 (Spring 1951): 425–39.

Meader, George. "Congressional Investigations: Importance of the Fact-Finding Process." *University of Chicago Law Review.* 18 (Spring 1951):449–54.

Melville, Charles H. "Legislative Control Over Administration Rule Making." *University of Cincinnati Law Review.* 32 (Winter 1963):33–54.

Millett, John D., and Rogers, Lindsay. "The Legislative Veto and the Reorganization Act of 1939." *Public Administration Review.* 1 (Winter 1941):176–89.

Morrow, W. L. "Legislative Control of Administrative Discretion: The Case of Congress and Foreign Aid." *Journal of Politics.* 30 (November 1968):985–1011.

Morstein Marx, Fritz. "Congressional Investigations: Significance for the Administrative Process." *University of Chicago Law Review.* 18 (Spring 1951):503–20.

Nelson, Randall H. "Legislative Participation in the Treaty and Agreement Making Process." *Western Political Quarterly.* 13 (March 1960):154–71.

Newman, Frank C., and Keaton, Harry J. "Congress and the Faithful Execution of Laws—Should Legislators Supervise Administrators?" *California Law Review.* 41 (Winter 1953–54):565–95.

Nieburg, H. L. "The Eisenhower AEC and Congress: A Study in Executive-Legislative Relations." *Midwest Journal of Political Science.* 6 (May 1962):115–48.

Patterson, Samuel C. "The Professional Staffs of Congressional Committees." *Administrative Science Quarterly.* 15 (March 1970): 22–37.

Perkins, James A. "Congressional Investigations of Matters of International Import." *American Political Science Review.* 34 (April 1940):284–94.

Perlmutter, Oscar W. "Acheson vs. Congress." *The Review of Politics.* 22 (January 1960):5–44.

Redford, Emmette S. "A Case Analysis of Congressional Activity: Civil Aviation, 1957–58." *Journal of Politics.* 22 (May 1960):228–58.

Rogers, Lindsay. "Congressional Investigations: The Problem and Its Solution." *University of Chicago Law Review.* 18 (Spring 1951): 464–77.

Rourke, Francis E. "Administrative Secrecy: A Congressional Dilemma." *American Political Science Review.* 54 (September 1960):684–94.

Scher, Seymour. "Conditions for Legislative Control." *Journal of Politics.* 25 (August 1963):526–51.

_____. "Congressional Committee Members as Independent Agency Overseers: A Case Study." *American Political Science Review.* 54 (December 1960):911–20.

Schneier, Edward. "The Intelligence of Congress: Information and Public Policy Patterns." *The Annals.* 388 (March 1970):14–24.

Schwartz, Bernard. "Executive Privilege and Congressional Investigatory Power." *California Law Review.* 47 (March 1959):3–50.

Sharkansky, Ira. "An Appropriations Sub-committee and its Client Agencies." *American Political Science Review.* 59 (September 1965):622–28.

_____. "Four Agencies and an Appropriations Subcommittee: A Comparative Study of Budget Strategies." *Midwest Journal of Political Science.* 9 (August 1965):254–81.

Shils, Edward A. "Congressional Investigations: The Legislator and His Environment." *University of Chicago Law Review.* 18 (Spring 1951):571–84.

Smith, Harold D. "The Budget as an Instrument of Legislative Control and Executive Management." *Public Administration Review.* 4 (Summer 1944):181–88.

Smith, J. Malcolm, and Cotter, Cornelius P. "Administrative Accountability: Reporting to Congress." *Western Political Quarterly.* 10 (June 1957):405–15.

Thomas, Norman C. "Bureaucratic-Congressional Interaction and the Politics of Education." *Journal of Comparative Administration*. 2 (May 1970):52–80.

Thomas, Robert D., and Handberg, Roger B. "Congressional Budgeting for Eight Agencies, 1947–1972." *American Journal of Political Science*. 18 (February 1974):179–85.

Vinyard, Dale. "Congressional Checking on Executive Agencies." *Business and Government Review*. 11 (September–October 1970): 14–18.

――――. "Congressional Committees on Small Business." *Midwest Journal of Political Science*. 10 (August 1966):364–77.

――――. "The Congressional Committees on Small Business: Pattern of Legislative Committee–Executive Agency Relations. *Western Political Quarterly*. 21 (September 1968):391–99.

Voorhis, Jerry. "Congressional Investigations: Inner Workings." *University of Chicago Law Review*. 18 (Spring 1951):455–63.

Weidenbaum, Murray L. "On the Effectiveness of Congressional Control of the Public Purse." *National Tax Journal*. 17–18 (December 1965):370–74.

White, Howard. "The Concurrent Resolution in Congress." *American Political Science Review*. 35 (October 1941):886–89.

――――. "Executive Responsibility to Congress via Concurrent Resolution." *American Political Science Review*. 36 (October 1942): 895–900.

White, Leonard D. "Congressional Control of the Public Service." *American Political Science Review*. 39 (February 1945):1–11.

Wildavsky, Aaron. "The Annual Expenditure Increment—Or How Congress Can Regain Control of the Budget." *The Public Interest*. 33 (Fall 1973):84–108.

――――. "TVA and Power Politics." *American Political Science Review*. 55 (September 1961):576–90.

Younger, Irving. "Congressional Investigations and Executive Secrecy: A Study in the Separation of Powers." *University of Pittsburgh Law Review*. 20 (June 1959):755–84.

Unpublished Sources Related to the Study of Legislative Oversight

Bibby, John F. "Legislative Oversight of Administration: A Case Study of a Congressional Committee." Ph.D. dissertation. University of Wisconsin, 1963.

Bozik, Edward Eugene. "National Defense and Congressional Behavior: Congressional Action on Authorizing and Appropriating Legislation for Military Budgets and Military Construction, 1951–1966." Ph.D. dissertation. Georgetown University, 1968.

Cunnea, Patricia E. "Water Resources Policy Formation in the Appropriations Process: Congress and the Bureau of Reclamation." Ph.D. dissertation. University of Chicago, 1963.

Fleer, Jack D. "Congressional Committees and the Making of Military Policy: Authorizations and Appropriations for Major Weapons Systems in the Legislative Process." Ph.D. dissertation. University of North Carolina at Chapel Hill, 1965.

Gawthrop, Louis C. "Congress and Foreign Aid: A Study of Congressional Control over the Administration of Foreign Aid Policy." Ph.D. dissertation. The Johns Hopkins University, 1963.

Goodsell, Charles True. "Congressional Access to Executive Information: A Problem of Legislative-Executive Relations in American National Government." Ph.D. dissertation. Harvard University, 1961.

Henderson, Thomas Arthur. "The House Committee on Government Operations and Congressional Oversight of Executive Agencies." Ph.D. dissertation. Columbia University, 1968.

Jahnige, Thomas P. "Congress and Space: The Committee System and Congressional Oversight of NASA." Ph.D. dissertation. Claremont Graduate School, 1965.

Johannes, John. "Statutory Reporting Requirements: An Assessment." Paper prepared for delivery at the Annual Meeting of the Midwest Political Science Association, Chicago, 1974.

———. "Study and Recommend: Statutory Reporting Requirements as a Technique of Legislative Initiative." Paper prepared for delivery at the Annual Meeting of the American Political Science Association, Chicago, 1974.

Keighton, Robert L. "The Executive Privilege and the Congressional Right to Know: A Study of the Investigatory Powers of Congressional Committees." Ph.D. dissertation. University of Pennsylvania, 1961.

Kolodziej, Edward A. "Congress' Use of Its Appropriations Powers to Determine Force Levels and Weapon Systems, 1946 to 1958." Ph.D. dissertation. University of Chicago, 1962.

LeLoup, Lance T. "Explaining Agency Appropriations Change, Success, and Legislative Support: A Comparative Study of Agency Budget Determination." Ph.D. dissertation. Ohio State University, 1973.

Levy, Arthur B. "Formal Techniques of Oversight: The Case of the

House Agriculture Committee, 1964–1965." Ph.D. dissertation. Harvard University, 1971.

Menge, Edward, Jr. "Congress and Agency Appropriations: An Explanation of House Appropriations Committee Actions for Federal Agencies." Ph.D. dissertation. Ohio State University, 1973.

Rundquist, Barry S. "Congressional Influences on the Distribution of Prime Military Contracts." Ph.D. dissertation. Stanford University, 1973.

Smallwood, Frank. "The Joint Committee on Atomic Energy: Congressional 'Watchdog' of the Atom?" Paper prepared for delivery at the Annual Meeting of the American Political Science Association, New York, 1962.

Stephens, Herbert W. "The Role of a Legislative Committee in the Appropriation Process: A Study Focused on the House Armed Services Committee." Ph.D. dissertation. The Florida State University, 1967.

Sturner, William F. "Aid to Yugoslavia: A Case Study of the Influence of Congress on a Foreign Policy Implementation." Ph.D. dissertation. Fordham University, 1966.

Index

Abell, Tyler A., 155–56
American Economic Association, 106
Amrine, Michael, 125
Ashmore, Robert, 147

Bailey, Stephen K., 200
Banking and Currency Committee: House, 34; Senate, 20–21, 182
Baran, Paul, 113–14
Belen, Fred, 172
Betts, Jackson, 171
Bibby, John F., 10, 182
Bolling, Richard, 19
Bowman, Raymond, 98, 108, 111
Bray, Bun, 30
Brim, Orville, 107
Brooks, Jack, 139
Brown, Louise Royster, 76
Broyhill, James T., 170
Bullock, Charles S., III, 57
Bureaucracy, accountability of, 191–92
Bureau of the Budget, 97, 98, 105, 106, 107, 108, 109, 110, 111, 112, 114, 115, 117, 194

Carp, Al, 119, 125
Celler, Emanuel, 129, 130, 131, 134, 135, 136, 137, 139, 141, 142, 144, 145, 146, 147, 148, 151, 184
Civil rights legislation. See Over-

sight of bureaucracy, congressional
Civil Service Commission, United States, 121, 125, 126, 127
Clapp, Charles L., 162, 213n
Committees in Congress: Banking and Currency, House, 34; Banking and Currency, Senate, 20–21, 182; Joint Committee on the Organization of Congress, 1966, 7, 131, 175, 179, 187, 188; Rules Committee, House, 140, 143, 146–47; Truman Committee, 195
—Government Operations Committee, House, 25, 59, 92–128; budget, 94, 189; chairman, 92, 94, 100–01, 104; executive branch, relations with, 102, 115; hearings, 117–21, 125–27; investigations, 105–17, 117–28; legal authority, 93–94, 115; partisanship, 102; seniority on, 101–02; staff, 94–96, 127; status on, 101–02; structure, 92–93, 99–101; subject matter and, 96–99, 112–15. See also Special Subcommittee on the Invasion of Privacy
—Judiciary Committee, House, 24–25, 59, 129–52, 189; assignment to, 138–39, 211n; budget of, 130–31, 141; chairman of, 130–31, 134, 135;

executive branch, relations with, 136–38; hearings of, 146–48, 148–51; investigations by, 140–41, 142–44, 144–48; legal authority of, 129–31; partisanship on, 135–36, 137; priorities of members, 131, 138–42, 144; school guidelines controversy and, 142, 144–48; special ad hoc advisory committee on civil rights and, 142–44, 146; staff of, 131–33; status on, 134–36; structure of, 134, 142–44; Subcommittee Five, 129, 134–35, 137, 138, 139, 140, 141, 148, 211n; subject matter and, 132, 133; workload of, 129, 130, 131–32, 140, 141, 144, 146, 211n

—Judiciary Committee, Senate, Subcommittee on Constitutional Rights, 123–28, 169, 183, 209n

—Post Office and Civil Service Committee, House, 24, 27–91, 92, 188, 195; assignment to, 41, 56–59, 211n; chairman of, 38–40, 42–44; executive branch, relations with, 44–54; legal authority of, 28–29; lobbying and lobbyists and, 27, 63, 64–91; Manpower Subcommittee, 30, 185; partisanship on, 42–43, 51–54, 61; pay bill, federal employees, 27, 62, 82–83; postal rates and, 82–83; priorities of members of, 36–38, 53–54, 56–91; reorganization of, 1965, 39–41, 43, 185; seniority on, 58, 63; staff of, 29–33, 84–85; status on, 41–44, 47, 63, 68; structure of, 38–41; subject matter and, 33–38, 48

Congress: decline of, 193; functions of, 7–9, 196–99; reform of, 18, 186–91, 196–202. *See also* Committees in Congress; Congressmen; Oversight of bureaucracy, congressional

Congressional Budget and Impoundment Control Act of 1974, 181

Congressional oversight of bureaucracy. *See* Oversight of bureaucracy, congressional

Congressional review. *See* Oversight of bureaucracy, congressional

Congressmen: priorities and incentives, 15, 19–21, 36–38, 53–54, 56–91, 102–05, 115, 128, 131, 138–42, 144, 177–78, 182–83, 185–86, 196, 201–02; workload and time, 14, 19, 58–63, 104, 131–32, 140, 141, 146, 159, 177

Conte, Silvio, 157

Corbett, Robert J., 67–68, 173

Corman, James C., 139, 142, 147

Cornish, Norman, 120–21

Cotter, Cornelius P., 175, 190

Cramer, William, 139, 147

Creech, William, 126

Cullinan, Gerald, 88–89, 90

Cunningham, Glenn, 66

Data bank, national. *See* Special Subcommittee on the Invasion of Privacy

Davidson, Roger H., 163, 188, 190

Dawson, William, 99, 100, 102, 119, 184, 185, 209n

Day, J. Edward, 157, 172

Dirksen, Everett M., 52

Donohue, Harold D., 139

Drury, Allen, 16–17

Dulski, Thaddeus J., 66, 70–71, 91, 166

Dunn, Edgar S., 106, 110

Dwyer, Florence P., 18

Eagle, Steven, 95

Ellsworth, Robert F., 170

Ervin, Sam, 123–24, 125, 126, 173–74

Fenno, Richard F., Jr., 10–11, 17, 23, 88, 216n
Ford, Gerald, 52, 57
Freedman, Monroe, 123, 124
Freeman, J. Leiper, 10, 160, 184
Friedrich, Carl J., 192

Gallagher, Cornelius E., 95, 97, 99, 100, 101, 102, 103, 104, 108, 109, 111, 113, 116, 118, 120, 122, 124, 125, 126, 168, 185, 209n, 210n
Gardner, John, 146, 158
Gawthrop, Louis C., 59
Gellhorn, Walter, 164
General Accounting Office, 12, 93, 192, 199, 218n
Government Operations Committee. *See* Committees in Congress
Green, William, 19
Gronouski, John, 48, 49
Gross, H. R., 170

Hall, Durward, 169
Harris, Joseph P., 7
Hatch Act, 68, 69
Hearings. *See* Committees in Congress; Oversight of bureaucracy, congressional
Henderson, David, 158
Horton, Frank, 101, 103, 104, 107, 108, 119–20
Howe, Harold, 147
Huitt, Ralph K., 153, 186, 212n
Huntington, Samuel P., 196–99, 200
Hyneman, Charles, 7

Incentives. *See* Congressmen: priorities and incentives
Invasion of privacy. *See* Special Subcommittee on the Invasion of Privacy

Investigations. *See* Committees in Congress; Oversight of bureaucracy, congressional

Javits, Jacob, 166
Johannes, John, 214n
Johnson, Albert, 34
Johnson, Byron L., 178
Joint Committee on the Organization of Congress, 7, 131, 175, 179, 187, 188
Jones, Jesse, 17
Judiciary Committee, House and Senate. *See* Committees in Congress

Kastenmeier, Robert, 134, 139, 142, 143, 146, 147
Kaysen, Carl, 107, 112
Keating, Jerome J., 78, 88, 89
Kennedy, Robert, 23
Kerlin, Don, 32
King, Martin Luther, Jr., 23
Kofmehl, Kenneth, 182
Kovenock, David M., 163, 188
Krebs, Paul, 42, 59

Legislative oversight of bureaucracy. *See* Oversight of bureaucracy, congressional
Legislative Reorganization Act of 1946, 5, 6, 12, 13, 29, 62, 93, 94, 188–89
Legislative Reorganization Act of 1970, 181, 189–90
Legislative review. *See* Oversight of bureaucracy, congressional
Lindsay, John, 139
Lobbying and lobbyists. *See* Committees in Congress; Oversight of bureaucracy, congressional
Long, Edward V., 169
Long, Russell, 158

Macy, John, 121–22, 125–26, 172

Manley, John F., 13
Mann, Barbara Laughlin, 177
Masters, Nicholas A., 58
Mathias, Charles, 139, 142
Matsunaga, Spark, 63, 78, 170, 171
McCulloch, William, 136, 139, 146
McGregor, Clark, 139
Monagan, John S., 93
Monroney, A. S., 12–13
Monroney-LaFollette Act. *See* Legislative Reorganization Act of 1946
Morrison, James, 44, 66, 174, 207n
Murray, Tom, 39, 59, 185

National Alliance of Postal and Federal Employees, 67, 69–70, 76
National Association of Letter Carriers, 65, 66, 67, 72–73, 75, 77, 78, 79–81, 86, 88, 89, 90
National Organization of Postal Supervisors, 67, 75
National Postal Union, 67, 75, 77, 81
National Rural Letter Carrier's Association, 75
New York City Bar Association, 7

O'Brien, Lawrence, 45, 46, 48, 49, 50
Obscenity in the mails, 36
O'Leary, Michael K., 163, 188
Olsen, Arnold, 32, 66, 165, 170
Oversight of bureaucracy, congressional: analysis of, research on, 4, 9–11, 11–22, 23–26, 48, 55, 181–86, 187, 188–89, 192–93, 193–95, 215n, 217n; bicameralism and, 124–28, 136, 183, 196; casework and, 148, 162–75, 198, 200, 213n; on civil rights legislation, 132, 133, 134, 136–37, 141, 142–44, 149–51, 192; committee structure and,

15, 38–41, 92–93, 99–101, 134, 142–44, 183–85, 187–88, 190; conversion factors leading to, 22–23, 105, 115–16, 182; definition of, 6–7, 11, 108, 155; executive branch relations and, 16–18, 44–54, 102, 115, 136–38, 160–61, 164, 167–68; hearings and, 7, 117–21, 125–27, 146–48, 148–51, 153–62, 212n, 213n; impact of, 105, 111–12, 116–17, 120–24, 185–86; investigations and, 105–17, 117–28, 140–41, 142–44, 144–48, 193–95; as latent function, 10, 26, 155–62, 166–71, 180, 186; legal authority for, 5, 11–13, 28–29, 93–94, 115, 129–31, 189, 217n; lobbying and lobbyists in, 27, 63, 64–91; as norm, 5, 181; norms and behavior and, 5, 93–94, 129, 181, 188; opportunity factors leading to, 11–22, 28–55, 90–91, 93–104, 112–15, 182; oversight calendar and, 190–91; partisanship and, 17–18, 42–43, 51–54, 61, 102, 135–36, 137; performance, quality of, 4–6, 10, 13, 105, 116–17, 123–28, 150–51, 186, 193–96; policy preferences and, 5–6, 22, 137–38; reform of, 18, 186–91, 196–202; reports required by Congress and, 175–80, 214n; staffs, committee and member, 13–14, 16, 29–33, 94–96, 127, 128, 131–33, 185, 199, 218n; status on a committee and, 16, 41–44, 101–02, 134–36, 169; subject matter and, 14–15, 33–38, 48, 96–99, 112–15, 133. *See also* Committees in Congress

Packard, Vance, 109, 116
Patterson, Samuel C., 206n
Perkins, Lynette P., 194

Personality testing. *See* Special
Subcommittee on the Invasion
of Privacy
Pois, Joseph, 199, 218n
Postal Reorganization Act of
1970, 91
Post Office and Civil Service
Committee, House. *See* Com-
mittees in Congress

Rademacher, James, 88
Redford, Emmette S., 183
Reports required by Congress. *See*
Oversight of bureaucracy,
congressional
Reuss, Henry D., 119, 212n
Robertson, Nan, 116, 171
Robinson, James, 16, 44, 166,
167
Rodino, Peter, 130, 139
Rogers, Byron, 130, 139, 147
Rosenthal, Benjamin, 96, 99, 101,
102, 103, 104, 110, 114, 126
Ruggles, Charles, 106, 107, 110
Rules Committee, House, 140,
143, 146–47

Saloma, John S., III, 4, 213n
Scher, Seymour, 6, 10, 20, 182
School guidelines controversy,
142, 144–48
Smith, Howard, 147
Smith, J. Malcolm, 175
Social Science Research Council,
106

Special Subcommittee on the
Invasion of Privacy, 92–128,
168, 183, 189, 192, 195;
national data bank and, 97–98,
105–17, 185, 195; personality
testing and, 96, 117–27, 183;
priorities of members of, 102–
05, 115, 128. *See also* Committees in Congress; Government
Operations Committee, House
Staff. *See* Committees in Congress;
Oversight of bureaucracy,
congressional
Steed, Tom, 155–56
Summerfield, Arthur, 207n

Truman, David B., 18
Truman Committee, 195
Tunney, John, 66, 170

Udall, Morris K., 66, 68, 78
United Federation of Postal
Clerks, 75, 78
United States Postal Service, 91,
192

Vinson, Fred, 16–17
Vinyard, Dale, 10, 174

Werts, Leo, 119–20
White, Leonard D., 193, 217n
Wilson, Charles, 66

Zwick, Charles, 117